MUSINGS
AND
ILLUSTRATIONS
IN
BLACK
&
WHITE
FROM
THE EDGE

A Compendium
Of
That Which Afflicts the Human Spirit

By
J. Wayne Frye

MUSINGS FROM THE EDGE: A COMPENDIUM OF THAT WHICH AFFLICTS THE HUMAN SPIRIT

The Author

Wayne Frye's Aaron Adams series, Girl books and Lynton adventures have been popular among Canadian mystery lovers since first appearing in 2005. He provides satirical political commentary to many Canadian newspapers, and his books on politics have created a great deal of controversy. He has written marketing/ advertising textbooks, been a successful U.S. university hockey coach, professor, university president and served as a marketing consultant to hockey teams and motion picture companies. He has been cited for his work with inner-city gang children in the Los Angeles area and been active in the anti-globalization movement. He became a Canadian citizen in 2003 and divides his time between Ladysmith, Vancouver Island, British Columbia and Cavite, Philippines.

Other Books by J. Wayne Frye

Hockey Mania and the Mystery of Nancy Running Elk
Something Evil in the Darkness at Hopkins House
How Hockey Saved a Jew From the Holocaust:
The Rudi Ball Story
The Catastrophic Calamities of a Village Idiot
Fighting for Justice in the Land of Hypocrisy
Guide to Alternative Education (13 Editions)
Cataclysmic Dreams in Black and White
Introduction to Advertising
Lynton Curls Her Hair
Lynton Buys a New Cell Phone and Hears the Voice of Doom
Lynton Walks On Water While Ingrid & Channa do an Irish Jig
Lynton and the Vampire at Tagaytay Manor
Fall From Apocalypse
Armageddon Now
Worth
When Jesus Came to Jersey as the Son of Thunder
The Girl Who Danced with the Demons of Darkness
The Girl Who Stirred Up the Whirlwind
The Girl Who Motivated Murder Most Foul
The Girl Who Said Goodbye for the Last Time
The Girl Who Made Love to the Yeti in Kathmandu
Canadian Angels of Mercy – Nurses in Times of Peril
Points of Rebellion: Aboriginals Who Fought for Justice
Chablis: Avenging Angel for the Forgotten
In the City of Lost Hope
Chablis and the Terrorist Who Resurrected the Spirit of Che

J. Wayne Frye

MUSINGS FROM THE EDGE: A COMPENDIUM OF THAT WHICH AFFLICTS THE HUMAN SPIRIT

TABLE OF CONTENTS

MUSINGS FROM THE EDGE: A COMPENDIUM OF THAT WHICH AFFLICTS THE HUMAN SPIRIT

TO:

All those who suffer in a world based upon greed where poverty is accepted so those at the top of the economic ladder can continue to live their lives of excess at the expense of those who toil in obscurity, and to the many who have loved passionately and paid a high price for it, but they should always remember that it is better to have loved and lost than not to have loved at all.
JWF

And as always to my muse
Lynton Globa Viñas

ISBN: 978-1-928183-05-1

Fireside Books – Victoria, British Columbia/Port Angeles, Washington
Peninsula Publishing Consortium

J. Wayne Frye

MUSINGS FROM THE EDGE: A COMPENDIUM OF THAT WHICH AFFLICTS THE HUMAN SPIRIT

INTRODUCTION

MEANING OF LIFE

In 2012, a newspaper article in a small town in England referred to me as an obscure Canadian writer. I always knew that I was not at the top of the best-selling authors, but I did once have a book that made it to number six in a specialized category on Amazon, so that word obscure really made me realize just how fleeting glory is for us all. We are born. We live, for most of us, fairly uneventful lives, and then we fade into obscurity. Lucky me, I got to read about my own obscurity before dying. If I were not planning on cremation and having my ashes placed in an urn that will set on the mantle in a whore house, I suppose I could have been like Chuck Jones who had the iconic words of his character Porky Pig carved on his tombstone – *That's All Folks*. Just imagine how wonderful it would be to lie in repose under the ground and have people laughing at the epitaph "Here lies an obscure man who was an obscure writer in an obscure town in an obscure house on an obscure island in British Columbia." There just seems something so final about that word obscure. It is as if our lives are meaningless in the grand scheme of things. The world is filled with people who love to aggrandize themselves. There are aristocratic families that somehow believe they are simply "entitled" by right of birth. The offspring of royal families, for the most part, really believe that they are ordained by God to be exalted. People like the Bush family, the Royal Family of England, the Middle Eastern Potentates, for some reason genuinely believe they are better than the average "Joe" who has to toil for a living.

I have spent most of my life proclaiming the ideal of parity of opportunity where all humans are afforded equal chances at a full and fruitful life, regardless of the circumstance of birth. Why should children born into poverty pay the heavy price exacted by a world based on greed so that those at the top can continue their economic dominance? In an economic world where capitalism rules supreme, those who do the work are rarely allowed to share in the fruits of their labour. Rather, most fortunes, be they individual or corporate, are built on the backs of the labourers. Those who really do the work are simply cogs in the giant machinery of capitalism where nepotism is built into the system so those at the top are protected and coddled and the wealth is passed on one generation to another.

Bring into this picture the word "love" and it appears that there may be a degree of equality in the world, because those who love, whether rich or poor, can soar to the heights of euphoria or descend into the abyss of misery regardless of their economic status. So when it comes to affairs of the heart, things are definitely more equal. However, as I used to tell my marketing students when I was a university professor, "The pursuit of money should not be the reason people live. It does not guarantee anyone happiness. However, when it comes to being miserable, it is easier to be miserable with money than without it."

In the hit 1970's television show *All in the Family*, Archie Bunker said once while arguing with his son-in-law about emotion, "The heart is the most emotional organ in the body." Most of us realize that there is no emotion in the heart, as it resides in the brain. Still, when we talk of love, it is referred to as an affair of the heart. I have had many affairs of the heart in my life. The first one being an infatuation, at the age of 5, with the little girl next door who would slip off into the forest behind our house with me and allow me to gently kiss her cheek. Of course, my young heart was broken when she moved away. And then there was my first grade romance with a pretty little thing named Judy, who was as sweet as a sugar cube, but she, too, changed schools when her family moved to another part of town. Alas, when we reconnected in high school, she had put me into the back corners of her mind, and showed no interest in a gangly, thin-as-a-rail, awkward boy with the savoir-faire of an Ostrich.

There were other amorous pursuits that worked out much better for me as I grew older. Some did not, of course. In fact, there were more that didn't than did. Along the way, there was also much heartache, because love is a fleeting thing. Just ask divorce lawyers and they can certainly attest to that fact.

I still carry a special place in my heart for the first girl who ever offered me the opportunity to experience sex.

MUSINGS FROM THE EDGE: A COMPENDIUM
OF THAT WHICH AFFLICTS THE HUMAN SPIRIT

After all these years, I am sure she would look back on her sexual peccadilloes with me as more amusing than erotic. However, like all adolescent experiences, it was part of a maturation process that frankly is still going on today as I edge toward my golden years. Do any of us ever really grow up? Well, maybe, but when I am too old to enjoy looking at a beautiful woman just throw the dirt over me, because I am undoubtedly already dead. Life is a mosaic of the possible in pursuit of the impossible. Can any of us ever really achieve nirvana? No, but the pursuit of it is great fun and it also fraught with some misery in the process.

What follows is a compilation of some of my most profound musings. Why are they profound? Because I say they are. I didn't say you had to agree. In fact, you may often disagree, but the fact that you are reading them means you are a person in pursuit of that which eludes the majority of us who live in that aforementioned obscurity to which I referred. The truth is that our obscurity is defined by those who do not know us. In truth, we are only obscure if we are not loved and if we do not know how to love. So, let's start on a journey where we will trample on economic, social and love obscurity in pursuit of the ever elusive "meaning of life."

J. Wayne Frye

PROLOGUE

LET'S ROCK AND ROLL

In Charlie Chaplin's famous movie, *The Great Dictator*, at its conclusion he issued a plea for people of good will to unite and pursue freedom. He begged for mercy from those who ruled. How wonderful it would be to live in a world where no one thought they had a right to conquer anyone else, a right to reign in luxurious splendour while relegating the vast majority to a life of economic servitude or to believe that by virtue of birth some are to be exalted over others. What a world it could be if only the hearts of those in positions of power and those with great financial wealth could have a bit of compassion. If people of influence cared more about the happiness of others, so much pain could be alleviated.

Why does the wealthy Christian person who proclaims fealty and undying belief in the Bible ignore Jesus' plea for the rich to give all they have to the poor? It is true that whoever loves money never has enough money. Some people are never satisfied with what they have. As Jesus said, "The love of money is the root of all evil." Notice he did not say money itself was evil, but the love of it was evil. And what of he or she who loves power and prestige? Power and prestige equals money, because power brings privilege and gets all wants satisfied. Look at the politicians whose privilege gives them huge incomes, parsimonious benefits and secure old age retirement while the vast majority of us toil in obscurity for a penance.

Whoever has money never has enough, and in a world where every country but one (Cuba) is based upon the principle of greed there is simply no hope for man to rise from the depths of despair imposed by those at the top of the economic and political ladder. Mao is, no doubt, turning over in his Beijing mausoleum as the country he founded on the principle of economic equality has now joined the United States in aggrandizing greed as an enviable trait. How horrible that the world embraces the idea that those at the top have the right to live in luxurious splendour at the expense of those mired in the misery of poverty.

Where is the church, the mosque, the synagogue, the temple or other places of worship when the hungry, those with no shelter, those with no job cry out and are rebuked? How can great edifices be built to glorify God, when his true glorification would be through the hand of compassion for those who are crying in the wilderness of despair? Rather than going to the houses of worship, true believers should be marching on the seats of government, demanding an end to foolish expenditures on war. They should be demanding a more equitable distribution of the wealth. They should be pressing governments to provide all with jobs, shelter and health care because all those things are possible in a world where greed is arrested, imprisoned, quarantined and crushed. Where were all these good religious people while the USA was busy torturing prisoners all across the globe and raining down bombs on innocent women and children? They deplored the loss of the 3,000 people on 9/11, but what of the over 5 million people killed by US bombs, bullets and wars all across the globe since 1965 in an attempt to secure the world for the government's corporate masters? Mao said that power comes from the barrel of a gun. The USA, with enough weapons to destroy the world 5 times over, is proof of that. No country and no individual are safe from the wrath of the United States of America. The staid religious institutions sit on the sidelines while allowing this carnage of human dignity to go unchecked and un-protested.

Man, as Chaplin said, has lost his way, but the way could be beautiful and free. Greed has poisoned the souls of mankind. Those few who are lucky enough to rise from poverty turn their backs on those whose fate they once shared. The accumulation of money does not have a corresponding accumulation of compassion. Man can soar to the heavens, but he cannot eliminate want on earth. Modern technology has made our lives easier, but at what cost to our freedom. How free are you when you are glued to that cell-phone provided by corporations that extract thousands of dollars from your pocket so that those in control can have their greed satisfied? Machinery may seem to provide abundance, but it only fuels the desire for more. Has all the advancement made by man really improved the human condition or just altered the conditions of our misery? Today, men think too much and feel too little. Without gentleness, kindness and generosity there is no hope in this world where greed rules supreme.

Technology is not all bad. It can be used to lift the human spirit. I volunteer for a help-line and by virtue of modern communications I was able to use a video call on my computer to spend five hours talking to a person who was ready to commit suicide. Today that person is breathing because technology allowed me to reach out to her. Like so many people, her biggest problem was lack of acceptance in a society that does too much finger-pointing and not enough loving. Yet, the real function of all technology is to generate income for our corporate masters and those at the top of the economic ladder. Does anyone really believe the purpose of television is to entertain? Television once brought culture to the masses, but the inane programming of today that is aimed at the mind of a 12 year old is nothing but a platform for corporations to get more customers to buy products and services they really don't need. With today's television, programs interrupt the commercials rather than the other way around. This is the way of the modern world where everything has a price tag.

I once believed in the 1960's that society was headed for an upheaval that would sweep away greed and introduce true freedom to a world that was embracing change, but the governments of the world, in collusion with corporations, brought that opportunity to a halt through intimidation, coercion, harassment and even imprisonment. Where are all the 60's radicals today? Most decided having a BMW, a house in the suburbs and a tidy pay check while 50% of the world still wallowed in poverty wasn't all that bad. They decided to cash in and look after themselves. They became part of the society of greed.

It is easier to despise than to love. Bitterness is a precursor to acceptance of your fate. It takes less effort to submit to your enslavement. Why think when you can get someone to do it for you? Why not become machine men, with machine hearts, machine minds? Why not become like cattle and be herded up into pens where you think your needs are satisfied? Think! Think! Where do cattle eventually wind up? Are not most people lining up and being led to their own slaughter?

Today's world is based on the sordid necessity of the underclass to serve the needs of the 2% at the top of the economic ladder. This underclass must actually always be expanding, because those at the top need more and more workers to dutifully and humbly serve them. Poverty is therefore institutionalized into any system based on greed. Those at the bottom are kept at bay with promises from government that equality of opportunity abounds and if one works hard there is always room at the top. The truth is that the top is only reserved for those who come from the families of the 1 % or 2% who get all the benefits in a capitalistic society. The occasional underclass person who gets to the top is held up as an example of the fairness of the system, when in reality, only a small number from the underclass ever make it out of poverty, because the stratospheric pinnacle of the rich is only reserved for those from the privileged class.

Converting private property into public wealth, and substituting co-operation for competition, would restore society to its proper condition of a thoroughly healthy organism, and insure the material well-being of everyone with no one forced to live on the margins. Poverty is often praised as a builder of character. How much character can be built in the belly of a two year who has to go to bed hungry at night, so a few can dine on caviar? Those at the top gain much in material prosperity from those who toil for meagre wages, but the poor are absolutely of no importance in a system based on greed. The system crushes those at the bottom, quickly forgets them when they are used up and discards them when they are of no more value as producers of wealth for the top 2%. The system crushes these people. Indeed, the system prefers people be crushed, as that makes sure the workers are far more obedient.

At my age, I have not seen the progression of man toward freedom, but the regression back to a tribal state. I long for a world where greed is not the cornerstone of existence, but rather, a world where equality reigns like a benevolent monarch of opportunity for all. I long for world of reason where progress is not measured in dollars and cents, but by the compassion and love we have for one another.

So, we now enter into the belly of the beast with this book which is an amalgamation of sorts that will be an introspection in regards to the social and economic climate that simply destroys most people and condemns far too many to a labyrinth of economic despair which in turn leads to emotional turmoil.

This is an exercise that examines the human condition and will concentrate on compassion lost, compassion sometimes found and the death of hope. I offer no apologies for the moroseness of many of the works presented herein, because the world is economically a very sad place for most, and it is not much better when emotions are taken into consideration, because as the old saying goes, misery loves company. So, saddle up, grab the reins and less rock and roll!

Capitalism at work!

KNOW the ENEMY

CAPITALISM is THE current dominant mode of production and manifestation of class society. It is omnicidal.

CHAPTER 1

THE SOCIAL COMMENTARIES

As mentioned previously, the human condition is fragile at best. The world of greed is filled with those who live on the edge, always on a narrow precipice ready to drop into the abyss of despair. So let's take a journey into a world where hope and promise seem ever elusive, a world where government serves the wealthy and shows disdain for the poor. The following poem was written when I was a member of the US Army at a time when there was no choice but to serve, because there was a draft. Actually, although I detested the military, as an intelligence analyst with a Top Secret Crypto security clearance, my eyes were opened about the truth in regards to the USA. I began to understand that for years I had swallowed the propaganda spewed out by the government in regards to the righteousness of America, when, in fact, it was the USA which was actually the biggest terrorist nation in the world, always resorting to bombs and bullets to solve any problem and to stop the spread of any ideology that was opposed to America's greed-based economic philosophy. It was a time of great awakening for me.

THE USED UP MAN

In the beginning, there was sanity,
only in small doses, but sanity nevertheless.
As time passed, my own mind deteriorated
into a mere shell of its former self,
until all the years of intensive study and learning
flowed into a river of mediocrity.
My mind razed by a cruel,
inhuman, warmongering system
of ineptitude and ignorance; once again,
I was worthy to walk among the exploited masses.
My mind and inner-self sacrificed at
the altar of patriotism and loyalty, I was safe.

Safe, for my ability to speak-out was captured, isolated,
torn out and exterminated along with my heart.
The will to resist was suppressed, abrogated,
picked to pieces until only a faint glimmer
of hope beat within my breast.
I had fallen prey.
Yes, prey to the most abominable, revolting, disgusting,
horrendous creature known to sane man,
a Frankenstein wilder than any nightmare
ever conjured up by Mary Shelly.
The U.S. Army wants you next.
It's had me. In fact, it's used me up.

U.S. Army at its best.
This isn't called
torture by the USA.,
but mere repetitive use
of legitimate force.

MUSINGS FROM THE EDGE: A COMPENDIUM
OF THAT WHICH AFFLICTS THE HUMAN SPIRIT

Americans are the most gullible people on the earth. They swallow a steady diet of propaganda telling them how free they are and how they are envied by the world. Neither is true. In fact, most of the world looks at the USA as a bully that is always trying to impose its will on others, and the only reason people immigrate to the USA is because it accepts more immigrants so the corporations can keep wages low. As for being free, if the citizens would take time away from *American Idol* and the other inane programs that pass as entertainment to read the Patriot Act, they would see that citizens of that country are always under surveillance and suspicion. In fact, of all the so-called democracies in the world, the USA comes the closest to being a police state. Many years ago, I wrote about what an empty shell this nation was.

SHE IS EMPTY

Under the skin of the Statue of Liberty
there are no lungs.
She gasps for air
she cannot possibly breathe.
What butcher zealously chopped up
this most holy American symbol of freedom?
Under the skin of the Statue of Liberty
there is no heart.
Gone, too, are the arteries of democracy
that pump into her the breath of life.
She is hung up bloodily, eyes a bulge,
like some gutted cow at the slaughter pen.
Only the hook is invisible.
She hangs and the dark shadow is cast over the land
Blotting out the sun
Jet crows circle over her body,

MUSINGS FROM THE EDGE: A COMPENDIUM
OF THAT WHICH AFFLICTS THE HUMAN SPIRIT

and at her feet the trees bend
in despair at her condition.
There is a thunder across the land.
There is a rumble beneath the shadow.
Flames from her torch drop on the avenue
at her feet like splashes of blood.
The masses run, hide, but reappear
to stand beneath the dark shadow.
The masses are thirsty, oh holy lie.
They have been inside liberty.
Horror, she is empty.

My military service opened my eyes to how America kept despots in power all over the world to further the aim of securing the world for exploitation by the capitalists who run the country. It was like I had been blind, but could finally see. All those years of propagandized manipulation seemed to flow into a raging torrent, as for

J. Wayne Frye

MUSINGS FROM THE EDGE: A COMPENDIUM
OF THAT WHICH AFFLICTS THE HUMAN SPIRIT

the first time I was able to see the sinister elements that were at play in the field of patriotic manipulation that was used to keep the populace in line. For that reason, I put pen to paper and composed the following.

THE REVOLTIONARY

The revolutionary must fight
against the winds of tyranny and force.
The revolutionary must take part
in the battle against the capitalists
who want to control all of humanity
in their pursuit of more and more.
The hypocrisy of the culture of greed
must be exposed so that all of humanity
can emerge from the dungeon of darkness and despair
into the bright sunshine of justice and equality.
The voices of the forgotten and disenfranchised
crying out for justice and reform must be heeded.
The evil of greed must be exposed so
it can no longer hide in the squalor of darkness,
turning its back with customary unconcern
to the plight of the masses.
If the house of ignorance continues to close its shutters
to this refreshing breeze of hope,
then the wind will become so violent and strong
that it will demolish the house
into a pile of worthless rubble.
It simply cannot stand against a righteous wind.
The revolutionary spirit must soar
in the hearts of all good men and woman
in a world that has lost its way
so that justice and freedom will reign
across the barren land of broken promises.

J. Wayne Frye   21

MUSINGS FROM THE EDGE: A COMPENDIUM OF THAT WHICH AFFLICTS THE HUMAN SPIRIT

The promise of America is an illusion, because those at the top of the economic ladder are always protected while those at the bottom are thrown tables scraps left over after the affluent have dined on the fatted calf.

THE TORCH OF HOPE

It is coming apart at the seams.
It is splitting in the middle.
The walls are crumbling.
The end is approaching.
It is falling into a deep, dark crevice
that is opening wider and wider
with each tick of the clock of doom.
The mighty of the mightiest, the holy of the holiest
is gasping for its last few breathes.
The final rights are already being murmured.
Yet, there are those who still refuse to let her die
as they cannot face the reality of death.
In a last attempt to save the graceful lady,
they turn their wrath on those
who know death is calling.
They lash out in anger at those
who proclaim death is inevitable.
In truth, she is not dying. She is not falling.
For that which never stood can never fall.
That which never lived can never die.
She was conceived in union,
but never emerged from her mother's womb.
She was a promise, a bold and holy promise
too noble for a generation of people
caught in the lust for wealth.
Yes, she can not die, because she never lived.
So let this symbol of hypocrisy pass on.

J. Wayne Frye

MUSINGS FROM THE EDGE: A COMPENDIUM
OF THAT WHICH AFFLICTS THE HUMAN SPIRIT

Let her fall into the decay and destruction
left by those who have profaned her
for she is only an unfulfilled dream.
It was a dream that eluded generations of people
in search of that which never really existed.
We must have a generation that is not beguiled
by an overly glorified past.
This generation must go inside liberty
and face the fact that she is empty.
That which never stood can never really fall.
The hypocrisy and deceit must end
and in its place we must find honesty,
decency and a new commitment to the idea of freedom
that will make it a reality for all Americans,
not just a chosen few.
Pass the torch to a new generation
dedicated to making
the country live up to its promise
of freedom, liberty and equality.
That torch can be used to burn and destroy
or it can be used to light the way
to a truly democratic, equalitarian society.

In 1981, I was the youngest university president in the United States of America, and I gave what is probably now considered one of the shortest commencement addresses ever, because I knew that the graduates were not interested in long-winded pontificating platitudes about what they had accomplished and how they were going to change the world. They wanted to simply get their degrees and head out into the world in pursuit of what everyone thinks brings happiness – money. Afterward, one student came up to me and said, "Dr. Frye, you shouldn't be president of a university, you should be in some Third World country leading a revolution."

I thought to myself, "Typical American response to the call for revolution. They only think other countries need a revolution. America is perfect." I turned to him and said, "No, if I was going to lead a revolution, it would be in the country that needs it the most, the USA."

1981 COMMENCEMENT ADDRESS BY WAYNE FRYE AT SOUHEASTERN UNIVERSITY NEW ORLEANS, LOUISIANA

"We just heard a speech extolling the virtues of America and its capitalistic system. The speaker had great praise for our new President. I have now discarded my prepared remarks and want to say a few words of rebuttal, and then I will get to handing out the diplomas, which may be my final act as president of this university, because I am about to ruffle many feathers with my remarks and may well be fired after this commencement. I defy you to name one piece of social legislation since Abraham Lincoln ever crafted by a Republican. They were against social security, the G.I. Bill, the Civil Rights Bill, Medicare, welfare, universal health care and every other piece of legislation aimed at assisting the working people of America. Lyndon Johnson once said, the only thing that Republicans were good at was investigating democrats and passing tax breaks for their rich friends. Today, with Ronald Reagan as President and his right-wing, conservative handlers pulling the strings, the state of the Republic is in grave danger of falling into the hands of people who will destroy the social safety net, hand the government over to anti-union capitalists, award obscene tax breaks to corporations and the wealthy, stifle truly democratic governments all over the globe through covert and overt intervention, support the repressive apartheid regime in South Africa, squander billions of dollars on needless military hardware and space-based weapons and muffle those in America who stand-up for the oppressed in a society that will be increasingly committed to widening the gap between the haves and have-nots."

"As I look out at you here today waiting to receive your hard-earned degrees, I urge you not to fall prey to this insidious, evil march to make the world into America, Inc. You will be tempted, bribed, cajoled, manipulated, and many times forced into accepting an unjust, unfair society as these barons of greed and right wing religious ideologues try to reshape America into the intolerant, self-aggrandizing, dissent-stifling nation that it became under the nearly Nazi-like years of the Nixon administration. You must stand fast against the coming tyranny that will be used by these warmongering, imperialistic, self-righteous hypocrites who think that America's divine destiny is to rule all of mankind under the banner of exploitive, corporate democracy."

"So, I make no long winded speech today, I just say come up and get your degree, and use it not to accumulate wealth for yourself, but use it to spread the knowledge of hope, charity and promise across a world that is rapidly falling prey to the evil of the aforementioned greed."

This obsession with the pursuit of wealth regardless of how many people must be trampled along the way, is the result of a world influenced by American dominance where capitalism is ballyhooed as the only workable economic system. Any system that supposes a fair distribution of wealth is not only economically unsound, but, according to the USA, is socialism, which rewards those who do not do their fair share. This preposterous assumption is used to keep Americans in service to an ideal that is inherently against most people's self-interest.

MUSINGS FROM THE EDGE: A COMPENDIUM
OF THAT WHICH AFFLICTS THE HUMAN SPIRIT

The following poem lays bare the insidious evil of a world that now enslaves us all to the corporate bottom line, and relegates everyone to be nothing more than a consumer who buys goods and services not needed so that 1% or 2% of the world's population can enjoy lives of splendorous excess.

A PRAYER TO THE CORPORATE GODS

Oh mighty global corporations
we are helpless without you.
Please bring your menial jobs to our cities and towns.
Though we have little control over these tedious jobs
that create wealth for the stockholders rather than us, they
are all that we lowly, shiftless, poor, useless workers
deserve from our benevolent benefactors.

Grant us your minimum wage per hour so that we may
have the hope of purchasing your fine,
cheaply-made products that we craft;
so that we can find that lasting contentment that only
comes from the possession of material things.
Forgive us when we question your authority,
or do not work fast enough or hard enough,
for we are but wretched servants who without your
generosity would be on the streets rather than living
in the houses that you allow us to rent from you
or to buy from banks that gouge us unmercifully.

Please drive us to serve you more diligently
until our broken bodies and spirits
are no longer of value to the corporation.
It is then that you should cast us out
with no concern, as what good are we?

J. Wayne Frye 27

MUSINGS FROM THE EDGE: A COMPENDIUM
OF THAT WHICH AFFLICTS THE HUMAN SPIRIT

when we can no longer toil for our corporate masters.

And great masters, when we are so destitute
and utterly penniless that we break
your commandments about stealing,
for we know you would never engage in thievery, please
protect your bounty by building walls and gates around
your homes so that we will not be tempted.

If we do backslide and break one of
your commandments, please put us
in a corporate operated jail so that we will at least know
that we are still serving the needs of stockholders as we
languish in our cold, concrete block cells
that we deserve for questioning your authority.

Of course, when we are in jail,
maybe you will let us be part of
the many corporate prison plans that allows you to pay
us a few cents an hour to work for you
to manufacture office furniture,
act as your call center or computer technicians.
O' great corporate Gods, thank you so much for giving
us the security of name brand products
made by cheap labour in deplorable conditions.
Without these brand names we would be nobody.
They give us true meaning in our worthless,
pitiful, utterly meaningless lives.

Also, please continue to spew your toxins and poisons so
that we can provide more corporations
with taxpayer dollars to clean up your mess.
We don't want clean water, pure food
or nasty old environmentally safe factories

J. Wayne Frye

that will take money out of your pocket.

We will gladly consume whatever you hand down
to us, for you are all knowing.
After all, the junk you define as food
is really good for us since we don't have
to bother to prepare it.
You put all those time-tested preservatives
in it to make sure it is safe.

O' great masters, please pacify us with your inane,
simple-minded plethora of prefabricated entertainment,
as we do not want any socially meaningful material
that might require us to think
or maybe even question your divine authority.

Reveal to us through your corporate controlled media
and pretty-faced, actor-newscasters what we
are to believe, for surely, we cannot trust our
own feeble judgment to lead us to enlightenment.
Please simplify our lives so that we can let you
do all our thinking for us.
Don't let us be challenged to think for ourselves.
This could well lead to anarchy and your downfall.

Most important, please guide your wise politicians
as they strive to make our lives better by passing laws
that eliminate worker's rights to keep us in line
and provide you with the tax cuts
that will keep you here.
Please, please don't leave us exalted ones.

Greed is like an incurable cancer that is constantly
gobbling up healthy cells to destroy all hope.

MUSINGS FROM THE EDGE: A COMPENDIUM
OF THAT WHICH AFFLICTS THE HUMAN SPIRIT

The USA prides itself on being a Christian nation, whatever that means. However, in doing so, it forgets one thing – the real Jesus. The below article was written to show just how hypocritical the Republican Party is. Of course, Republicans do not hold a monopoly on hypocrisy. It is very evenly distributed to other parties as well.

REPUBLICANS WOULD NOT
ELECT JESUS CHRIST
BECAUSE HE WAS A SOCIALIST

Jesus Christ did not give those hungry people fishing poles and bait. He gave them fish. He did not tell the people to go out and bake bread. He gave them bread. This, according to Republican doctrine would make him a Socialist.

Jesus Christ would not have told people to shut up and get to work without offering them the knowledge through education they needed to accomplish the task. He would not have callously let the children of the poor needlessly die from hunger and neglect in a world with an abundance of food. He would not have selfishly told the sick to heal themselves, because he wasn't going to give them access to a doctor or his healing touch. He would not have cut welfare, because he wanted to let the rich keep more of their money.

How hypocritical for the Republicans to claim they are the party of family values that wants to protect traditionalism and look to Jesus Christ as their model. These are the people who encourage the out-sourcing of American jobs to third world countries where

J. Wayne Frye

environmental concerns are minimized, child labour camps and near slave labour abound so corporations can ignore environmental safeguards and human rights to maximize profits. And, of course, one of the greatest lovers of Jesus is George W. Bush, noted torturer.

In America, Jesus would lose any election, because he would be branded a wild-eye anarchist rebel-rousing socialist, or even worse, a God-hating Communist. My suggestion to him would be to run for office in countries like Norway, Sweden, Finland, Denmark, France, Germany, Australia and Canada where supporting fair taxation, controlling corporate dominance, backing universal health care and protecting the marginalized members of society is the primary function of government. Granted, these countries are not perfect, but they do embrace compassion, unlike America, where a long-haired, sandal wearing, bearded man in ragged clothing like Jesus would have the church door slammed in his face.

One of the greatest men who ever lived is immortalized on T-shirts all over the entire world. How ironic that a man who saw capitalism as the chief impediment to progression toward freedom and equality would be used as a marketing tool to bring billions of dollars into the capitalists' coffers. The image of Che Guevara is probably one of the most recognizable images in the world.

It was during my military service that I sat at my Pentagon desk outside the office of the Joint Chief of Staff for Intelligence and listened to disparaging remarks that were directed toward Che Guevara, who had often been described by those who knew him as the most complete human being they had ever met. These career military people promulgated a lie about freedom and democracy in America, but Che knew the truth and understood that the USA was the chief impediment to peace because it used its power to keep despots in control in country after country. The only requirement was to be an anti-communist. It made no difference if you tortured, denied people their inalienable rights, imprisoned opposition leaders or rigged elections as long as you stood with America against what Ronald Reagan termed "the evil empire."

When I took over as director of the intensive academic support program with Los Angeles Unified School District, I was constantly appalled at how many of the ghetto children did not even know who the hero of the poor and downtrodden, Che Guevara was. This was a man who should be revered by the poor.

Hardly knowing the man; other than the stories I had heard about the CIA arranging his assassination in Bolivia, and how he had become disillusioned with Castro, when he felt the revolution had been betrayed, I decided to learn more about the man Americans had been taught to hate as a vassal of communist evil.

After a great deal of study and reflection, my respect for this great idealist who forsook a life of wealth and leisure in Argentina for the role of revolutionary and advocate for the poor made me realize even more what a hypocritical pack of deceivers were running America. For that reason, I decided to write a choral poem. It was brought to the stage in 1995, as part of a play.

MUSINGS FROM THE EDGE: A COMPENDIUM OF THAT WHICH AFFLICTS THE HUMAN SPIRIT

THE BALLAD OF CHE GUEVERA
ODE TO A REVOLUTIONARY

Che Guevara was a man of might,
Fighting for the oppressed day and night,
Giving his life for those who in poverty cried.
Oh, how the man fought and died.

Those times were extremely idyllic.
We looked for heroes to admire.
Then, out of the land of Argentina,
Came a man with eyes of fire.

Trained as part of the aristocracy,
He was taught to heal the tired and sick.
Yet, he knew medicine could not heal poverty,
And well over half of humanity did it afflict.

Filled with love for the downtrodden and forgotten,
While the corporate barons were cruel and cold,
He turned his back on luxury and affluence
To pursue revolution for fairness so bold.
He found a kindred spirit in the Caribbean,
Another revolutionary raging against the machine.
Fidel Castro was battling corporate oppression,
So to the jungle came Che, spirit so keen.

On the isle of Cuba, Che led the fight
Against Batista and American corporate greed.
With Castro by his side, victory was assured.
Yet, he wanted many others to be free.

Disillusioned by many revolutionary betrayals,
Che looked south for hope of his ideal.

J. Wayne Frye

MUSINGS FROM THE EDGE: A COMPENDIUM
OF THAT WHICH AFFLICTS THE HUMAN SPIRIT

Off to Bolivia to fight for what is right,
Where tyrants, people's freedom did steal.

Bolivia's masses were in pain for sure.
As supported and backed by America's might,
Corporations raped the land of minerals,
Suffocating people's inalienable rights.

Che's revolutionary reputation gave people hope.
Bolivia's generals slunk and cowered in fear.
America's CIA supported the oppressors in kind,
Letting the smisery continue without concern or care.

American policy said the people be damned.
Found and turned over to his deadly fate,
With CIA approval, the generals slew a dream.
But his legend they could not abate.

Whenever people pine and yearn for freedom,
Wherever they fight for right,
Che's name will live forever,
In the battle against the arrogance of might.

His name is far mightier
Than those who brought him down.
When are all relegated to the dust bin of history,
But Che will forever be wear his revolutionary crown.

Che Guevara was a man of might,
Fighting for the oppressed day and night,
Giving his life for those who in poverty cried.
Oh, how the man fought and died.

MUSINGS FROM THE EDGE: A COMPENDIUM
OF THAT WHICH AFFLICTS THE HUMAN SPIRIT

The USA is a nation that prides itself on being just, but in reality, it is a nation that has rarely been just when dealing with certain ethnicities and socio-economic groups. In fact, it has openly practiced genocide. The Native Americans were looked upon as backward savages, and official government policy from putting bounties on the heads of Native Americans to herding them into concentration camps that were benignly named reservations are prime examples of the hypocrisy that has been practiced over the years. The following poem illustrates how these noble people were robbed of their birthright when the European hordes stole their land and introduced the theory of ownership to people who had no concept of what that meant, since they believed that land could not be owned, as it was provided by the Great Creator for use by all. Chief Massasoit said, *"What is this you call property? It cannot be the earth, for the land is our mother, nourishing all her children, beasts, birds, fish and all men. The woods, the streams, everything on it belongs to everybody and is for the use of all.*

WHO IS THE REAL SAVAGE?

Where we walk each day,
Indian children used to play,
All about their native land,
Where shops and houses now stand.

These noble ones were driven away,
Never to return to former glory.
Today, they live in dismay,
On reservations in poverty they lay.

Why did this happen you ask?

J. Wayne Frye   35

MUSINGS FROM THE EDGE: A COMPENDIUM OF THAT WHICH AFFLICTS THE HUMAN SPIRIT

It truly should be told,
They were forced to leave, because
They did not fit the white man's mould.

Where are these people now?
Stuck on Reservations of broken land,
And expected to grow crops on desolate sand,
Because the country was stolen from them.

Beaten down and humbled by their fate,
I do not understand what makes whites insinuate
That these Native Kings and Queens are savages,
When it is the greedy, haughty whites with all the hate.

I have always taken a very serious and studious approach to the problems of society. My passion for hockey, both as a player later in life and as a coach, has made me aware competition is not bad. Competitiveness is a part of everyone's life to some degree. In 2001, I used hockey as a metaphor for the competitiveness in a capitalistic society that always leads to winners and losers.

CAPITALISM ON ICE

It was the season of light.
It was the season of darkness.
It was the season of hope.
It was the season of misery.
As I skated up the ice,
the puck on my stick was like a missile,
aimed at a foreign land.
I would launch it toward
that dreaded enemy, the goalie;

filling his net with the horror
and destruction of defeat.
I was the juggernaut of carnage.
As the puck skirted between his legs,
I knew that hockey was capitalism on ice.
My victory was his defeat.

Americans are constantly propagandized with platitudes about how great the USA is and how all others nations envy it, and, of course, the capitalist system based on greed is promoted as offering everyone an equal opportunity. That is far from the truth, as most nations see the USA as hypocritical and exceedingly violent. As for the capitalist system offering equality of opportunity, if it were not for the poverty induced by this system, it would indeed offer opportunity, but the poor serve a purpose – they do the work!

RATTA-TAT-TAT
SOUNDS OF THE HOOD

Ratta-tat-tat, Ratta-tat-tat.
The sounds of anger down in the hood.
Brothers killing brothers, it ain't no good.
America's got a damnable future for sure,
unless the power structure learns to be pure.

Ratta-tat-tat, Ratta-tat-tat.
It don't matter what colour you are.
Fighting over colours, your character will mar.
Telling home boys not to come to your school.
What made you bangers think you're so cool.

Ratta-tat-tat, Ratta-tat-tat.
Your butt will soon be a sling or dead.

MUSINGS FROM THE EDGE: A COMPENDIUM
OF THAT WHICH AFFLICTS THE HUMAN SPIRIT

Why don't you listen to what your mother said?
Tell me what you are going to say.
When you get home, you'll act a different way.

Ratta-tat-tat, Ratta-tat-tat.
You can be something, if you would.
But they ain't making it easy in the hood.
The future could be bright.
Wake up kid and see the light.

Ratta-tat-tat, Ratta-tat-tat.
Just let that awful sound die,
Fade away into a faint cry.
You got what it takes to succeed.
Determination is what you need.

Ratta-tat-tat, Ratta-tat-tat.
The sounds of anger down in the hood.
Brothers killing brothers, it ain't no good.
America's got a damnable future for sure,
unless the power structure learns to be pure.

Ask most Americans and they will extol the virtues of their country, because just like Nazi Germany during World War II, the government of the United States of America actively promotes patriotic indoctrination for all citizens, especially impressionable children. As a child in school, I was forced to stand and say the pledge of allegiance, which ironically, before World War II incorporated the Nazi salute as part of the process.

Searching for justice is a lonely journey. This pursuit has often brought me pain and misery, but to be true to myself it must continue. Remember what Che Guevara

J. Wayne Frye

said, "If you tremble with indignation at every injustice, then you are a comrade of mine."

CHAPTER 2

SEARCHING FOR TRUTH
IN A WORLD OF LIES

The following prose illustrates just how much devastation and misery can be wrought on those who dare challenge the American way of promulgating the corporate culture of greed. For those who dare stand against its tyranny are considered impediments to the corporate agenda that the USA represents. As Mitt Romney famously said in the 2012 U.S. Presidential election, "People are corporations, too."

True, people own stock, but the majority of the stock is owned by a few individuals who control things; consequently, the corporations are entities that represent the basest instincts of humans. So, corporations are people just like Mitt Romney, who inherited wealth, led a life of privilege and had a spot at the top of the corporate structure reserved for the scion of a wealthy man. His road to success had already been paved for him when he popped out of his mother's womb. We should all be so lucky.

MUSINGS FROM THE EDGE: A COMPENDIUM
OF THAT WHICH AFFLICTS THE HUMAN SPIRIT

So, I share now a few musings on the economic condition those of us who are of moderate means are expected to endure, so the few can continue gorge themselves at the table of plenty while the rest of us are thrown their leftovers.

A SYTEM THAT SEEKS TO ENSLAVE THEM

A few years ago, I decided to immigrate to Canada in search of a more just and humane society in order to free myself from the fascism taking hold south of us. Getting $1.51 for every U.S. dollar I brought into Canada, I deduced that I could have a nice, but not lavish, retirement in a country where healthcare was a right rather than a privilege, where the rich were not afforded unfair tax-breaks, where protecting the social safety net was considered the duty of a government that served the people rather than special interests and where bombs and bullets were not used as a tool to force other countries into submission. For a few short years, I thought I was rich. Then, George Bush's insane military adventures, economic incompetence and coddling of the corporations and wealthy, brought my economic security to a halt as I watched my monthly U.S. retirement checks dwindle down to as low as 91 cents Canadian to the U.S. dollar. Meanwhile, my savings were trapped in banks that were only willing to pay 1% interest while inflation soared at an official 3%, but, was in fact, more likely between 8% to 10%. It does not take a mathematical genius to figure out that my economic viability has been seriously threatened. Meanwhile, the jerk who set all this in motion is drawing a huge U.S. government pension and laughing all the way to the bank. Additionally, the disappointing, spineless coward who replaced him did nothing but acquiesce to the demands of the Republican Party that continued to believe in trickle down economics that allows we peons to fight for scraps from the table of plenty reserved for their corporate and wealthy benefactors.

I have the good fortune to be a Canadian citizen, so I know that I will not go without healthcare, shelter and something to eat. However, I spent my life scrimping and saving so I could accumulate a nest egg for my old age, and hopefully accumulate a little something to leave my children. However, in a world based on greed, the barons of capitalism have been allowed to rape, pillage and plunder those of us with moderate means. I actually consider myself fortunate, because I do have a few assets and a dollar or two left to last me for the few years I have remaining. However, for those with more modest means, I fear that the world is going to be increasingly divided into the haves and have-nots. The days of serfdom are returning with a vengeance, and the serfs are too complacent and demoralized to rise up in rebellion against a system that seeks to enslave them.

THE LAND OF BROKEN PROMISES

As the number of Americans saying good-bye to the USA increases, those of us who made this life changing decision years ago are wondering why so many waited so long to join those of us who have found serenity and peace in places where greed and lack of compassion are nothing but memories relegated to a dark corner of the mind. It is estimated that up to 15 million Americans will be voicing their discontent by simply leaving the country during the next 10 years. Most of them will be middle class and upper middle class professionals who have simply had enough of a society run by and for those at the top while those in the middle and lower classes are relegated to lapping up the scraps from the tables of plenty. The lower middle class and poor would join the exodus, but they have neither the skills nor the finances to afford throwing off their shackles and taking up residence in a more compassionate country.

In the past, many people left the United States of America in search of a better climate, a cheaper place to make their dwindling dollars go further or in search of the idyllic place to retire so they might enjoy their golden years. However, today's expatriates are, by and large, leaving simply because they have lost faith in the hope that things will get better. Some people are actually smart enough to realize the American dream is now a nightmare with the wealthy and corporate monsters devouring all hope. Most people are too scared to wake up and see the truth lurking in the darkness.

After 9/11, the deterioration of the USA, which had been occurring since the election of Ronald Reagan, began in earnest when the economy, political establishment and military were all hi-jacked by the corporate bottom-feeders who were given carte-blanche by a group of citizens who decided that sacrificing liberty to fight terrorism was acceptable. The fact that the government had shredded the Constitution was considered a small price to pay for safety. Meanwhile, the economy was deregulated, so Wall Street and the bankers could fleece people with impunity. The election of a supposed champion of the people (Barrack Obama) did nothing to change the equation, as he capitulated time-after-time to the forces of darkness that were determined to reintroduce the feudal system to modern America.

The political system is not just broken. It is corrupted. Corporations control the elections, not only with large donations now that the Supreme Court has ruled it is an abridgment of free speech to not allow these monotheistic monsters of mayhem to buy elections, but they even produce the voting machines that count the votes. Talk about letting the fox guard the hen house.

The judicial system, like every thing else in America, is there to serve the interests of the wealthy and powerful. The Supreme Court, with the exception of the minority liberals, protects the corporate evil-doers and the government fascists. Meanwhile, the corporate owned mainstream media spews out a steady diet of government propaganda in order to manipulate the public. Is it any wonder that so many Americans are trying to flee all this insanity?

With the Supreme Court appointment of George Bush as President in 2000, and the almost immediate economic meltdown that destroyed my stock portfolio after his tax breaks for the rich was passed, I decided to seek a place where health care was a right, not a privilege, and where people were a bit more pro-active and demanded that their government serve them, rather than corporations. In 2003, I crossed the border into Canada, and I have never looked back. My retirement income is tied up in the USA, so my assets are dwindling day-by-day, but, at my age, I know that I have enough to last until I die. I have no regrets, other than the fact that my children will now inherit much less. However, with the way things are going, even had I stayed, all my assets would have been gobbled up in a desperate attempt to survive in a society with no social safety net and no human compassion. I have had two strokes since coming to Canada. Had I been in the USA, where quality healthcare is based on dollars and cents, rather than compassion, my medical bills would have destroyed my economic viability and they care I would have received would have been mediocre. My on-going drug therapy alone would have been over $1200 a month in the USA. In Canada, not only was my hospitalization and doctor bills free-of-charge, but my drugs are all covered after a small deductible.

In today's America, people are slaves and they do not even know it. As they buy the latest electronic devices, as they ride around in their $50,000 cars, as they dine in expensive restaurants, as they struggle to make mortgage payments on houses they cannot afford, as they shake their heads in disbelief at the prices in corporate owned grocery stores, as they stand in blind obedience to a sing the National Anthem of a nation that is living a lie, they are putting their own shackles on to serve corporate masters who are laughing all the way to the bank.

I fondly remember the 1960's when the youth of America took to the streets, to not only stop an immoral war, but to demand social justice. These were people with ideals. These were people who wanted charity to rule over greed. They had compassion and genuine feeling for their fellow man. Yet, while America committed war crimes in Iraq and Afghanistan, while it tortured prisoners as young as 15, while it ran a gulag at Guantanamo, the American people were glued to their TV's watching *American Idol* or some other banal television pabulum that passes as entertainment in today's lowest common-denominator mass appeal world. Where are the individuals of conscience? The people today boo gay soldiers on national television and cheer when a Republican Presidential candidate who suggests someone without corporate provided health insurance should simply be allowed to die. This is the mentality of a nation that has lost its heart and soul tot eh culture of greed that is as pervasive as an ancient plague.

I have watched many of my fellow revolutionaries from the 60's fall victim to the pursuit of the all-mighty dollar and the happiness it is supposed to offer. Yet, I know there are good and decent people left in America, but it seems they are always being drowned out by those who think compassion has no place in a society where it is every man for himself. Which lead me to a simple question, what good is the pursuit of riches when you have to sacrifice your values in the process?

Like me, there are still some people in the USA who feel betrayed by the insidious evil of a system that serves the few at the expense of the many. However, the thought of leaving the familiar behind frightens people who have been fed a steady diet of how the USA is so superior to other societies. The very country that showed such disdain for the propaganda spewed out by the communists during the Cold War is completely blind to their own propaganda machine that starts with school age children being made to stand and recite the pledge of allegiance to begin each school day. Yet, I was able to overcome that engrained patriotism that makes slaves of so many to an ideal that exists only on paper, while the reality is just the opposite of what we were taught.

J. Wayne Frye

MUSINGS FROM THE EDGE: A COMPENDIUM
OF THAT WHICH AFFLICTS THE HUMAN SPIRIT

Canada is not a perfect place. The evil tentacles of the corporate culture exported by the USA all over the world reach here, too. Like the USA, the wealthy and powerful have great sway and influence, but if they go too far, the people here will not tolerate the inhumanity that is so common in the USA. Canadians look at their government differently. Unlike the USA, questioning the government is considered an act of patriotism. We, too, elect conservative governments on occasion, because there are five major political parties, and four of them are left-wing. Consequently, a conservative government can be formed with less than 25% of the vote sometimes. Yet, even conservative governments, like the one recently elected in Alberta, are committed to defending universal healthcare and the social safety net. This is a culture, unlike the USA, where the human equation is paramount. Food, shelter and health care are human rights in Canada. So, whether you chose Canada, or one of the other progressive social democracies, do not be afraid to turn your back on a country whose time has come and gone. Escape America before those in power erect more physical and psychological barriers that will imprison you forever in the land of broken promises.

MORE GOVERNEMENT DOES NOT
MEAN LESS FREEDOM

The vast majority of public programs do little to threaten the liberty of Americans. But it would be naive to ignore the fact that democratic governments can sometimes step over the line and pass laws that do violate people's basic rights and civil liberties. Consider the political witch-hunts of the McCarthy era in the 1950s, the FBI's harassment of civil rights leaders and the

Army's spying on the anti-war movement in the 1960s, and Nixon's "enemies list" and the Watergate scandal in the 1970s. More recently, in the wake of the 9/11 terrorist attacks, President Bush and the Republican Congress took a number of actions, including passing the Patriot Act, which undermined basic rights and freedoms while the ignorant masses cheered. The government greatly increased wiretapping and other forms of surveillance of citizens, often without any evidence of any wrongdoing on their part. Thousands of people were secretly detained for months without any charges against them. Suspected terrorists were denied lawyers and the right to a trial. Some suspects were even sent abroad to other countries so they could be tortured. And 2005 and 2006 revealed the existence of extensive domestic spying programs by the National Security Agency and other institutions that are legally forbidden from doing so, a very disturbing development. All this from the conservative Republicans who want less and less government, but have no trouble with government controlling women's bodies, using government to torture people and approving vast amounts of welfare for corporations while denying welfare for the poor. All of these violations of freedom, along with the cruelty of a system that makes healthcare a privilege rather than a right in the most hypocritical and warlike country on the planet, drove me to finally throw up my hands in disgust and immigrate to Canada. Now, I watch in disbelief as Americans are about to once again elect a man President who advocates the continuation of the insane Reagan-Bush policies that have caused all the agony that the USA is now facing. Mitt Romney is nothing more than a corporation in a suit. Believe me, I am no fan of Obama, because, unlike the Republicans, I see him for what he is - not a socialist, but a die-hard capitalist who capitulates to conservatives on almost every issue.

For the conservative government-haters, I ask you to consider this: Who comes to the rescue when the government violates peoples rights in the aforementioned ways? To whom do Americans turn to revoke or remedy those actions and to make sure that they don't happen again? The government. Sometimes the government acts independently in this protective role, as when federal authorities intervened in the 1960s when some states were violating the civil rights and voting rights of African Americans. But often it is citizens themselves who use one part of the government – usually the courts – to stop another part of the government from infringing on their freedoms and rights. Citizen organizations like the American Civil Liberties Union have been particularly active in using the courts to protect freedom of speech, freedom of religion, the right to vote, etc. Of course, the conservative Republicans decry the ACLU as nothing but a socialist nuisance to unfettered capitalism and the continued incarceration of people in the corporate run jails. Any organization that is concerned with protecting the poor and powerless is socialist according to these corporate, Jesus-loving hypocrites. Anyone with a grain of intelligence, who reads the Bible, could easily see that Jesus was a socialist. That is the real reason he was crucified. The Republicans are the modern Pontius Pilot's.

Americans, then, depend heavily on the tools of democratic government to protect people's rights. When they want to limit the abusive activities of government – such as unreasonable searches or unfair appropriations of property – they need to rely on the positive actions of another part of the government to do so. This is a point that anti-government conservatives consistently ignore. Yes, government can violate rights, but democratic government also functions as the main protector of rights and freedoms as well – and it has often done so very effectively in nations where there is compassion for the unfortunate. Certainly totalitarian and dictatorial governments are the enemies of freedom, but democratic governments have constitutions and institutions that enable them to effectively protect rights and freedoms.

People often make the mistake of seeing rights and civil liberties as merely the absence of some kind of governmental action. They firmly and irrevocably believe that there is free speech or freedom of religion when the government does nothing to impede those freedoms. But in reality, the people's rights depend heavily on active government – on positive government actions. In fact, the very existence of rights depends on government. In a very real way, rights and civil liberties are actually political constructs – creations of government. Formal rights do not exist until they are created by law or established in a constitution. Americans only have the right of free speech because it is guaranteed in the constitution. If they didn't have their constitution, or if they didn't have government, civil liberties would literally not exist. In a document which very few Americans know anything about, the preamble of the Constitution, the founding fathers did not say that in order to "secure liberty for ourselves and our posterity" they were going to abolish government; they said that they were going to "ordain and establish" a democratic constitutional government to do so. They knew that in democracies representative institutions do not steal liberties from people; they are the precious medium through which all secure their liberties.

MUSINGS FROM THE EDGE: A COMPENDIUM
OF THAT WHICH AFFLICTS THE HUMAN SPIRIT

Rights and liberties are not only created by people working through government, they rely on government to enforce them and create remedies for their violation. The traditional distinction that conservatives make between "negative rights" and "positive rights" is mistaken. Supposedly, negative rights, such as freedom of speech, simply require that the government not interfere with some activity. In this view, it is only positive rights, such as the right to health care, that require a government action to realize them. In fact, all rights require government action. They all require an active and well-funded government to enforce them – to make them real. Without a well-functioning legal and court system, for instance, the people's rights would be unenforceable and meaningless. Rights and freedoms, if they are to mean anything, require a vigorous response by government whenever they are violated. Every effort to prevent the government or private organizations from violating rights must be supported by court rulings, injunctions, damage awards, etc. Can you imagine a world where governments have no controls whatsoever over the corporations? Granted, politicians are bought by the corporations, but, at least, the bureaucrats have a few rules that can keep these monoliths of evil from the complete destruction of the planet. Without these bureaucrats, we would all be at the complete mercy of the behemoths of mischief.

Personal liberty cannot be secured merely by limiting government interference with freedom of action and association. No right is simply a right to be left alone by public officials. All rights are claims to an affirmative governmental response. All rights, descriptively speaking, amount to entitlements defined and safeguarded by law. A cease-and-desist order handed down by a judge whose injunctions are regularly obeyed is a good example of government "intrusion" for the sake of individual liberty. If rights were merely immunities from public interference, the highest virtue of government would be paralysis or disability. But a disabled state cannot protect personal liberties, even those that seem wholly "negative," such as the right against being tortured by police officers or prison guards. Granted, with Republican judges, torture and coercion are routinely accepted when applied against the poor and powerless, but through a system of appeals, there is always hope that a non-Republican judge might intervene and offer some justice. It almost seems that being heartless is a requirement to be a Republican.

Protecting and enforcing individual rights in this way is no small job. Think of all the various rights now taken for granted: the right to a fair trial, the right to own property, parental rights, voting rights, the right to not be denied a job because of race or gender, landlord and tenant rights, the right to run for office, the right to practice religion, mineral rights, consumer rights, the right to a minimum wage, the right to marry, copyright protections, the right to an attorney, the right to collect a debt, abortion rights, the right against self-incrimination, the right to free speech, the right to emigrate, intellectual property rights, the right to strike, the right to petition government, the right to privacy, child custody rights, the right to a safe workplace, the right to be free from illegal searches, and so on. Interpreting and enforcing all of these rights requires an extensive network of administrative and judicial organizations on the federal and state levels – courts, attorney generals' offices, civil rights agencies, even welfare agencies, etc.

These large governmental efforts cost billions of dollars a year – money that must come from taxpayers. In other words, rights depend heavily on an active and well-funded government. Without government spending all the world's economies would collapse. When governments find themselves in a position where they can't effectively tax and spend, citizen rights and liberties become unenforceable and largely non-existent. So, the function of government should be to level the playing field so all individuals have a fair shot at realizing economic independence, but corporate culture interferes.

In short, while we often think of our rights as freedom from government; in fact, we rely on an active government to establish and maintain those rights. This fact is indicative of the complete escape from reality practiced by those virulently maniacal anti-government conservative ideologues who always want to slash taxes and reduce government which is a direct contradiction in their claims to also value individual liberties. These throwbacks to the Middle Ages cannot understand that it is implausible to be for rights and against government.

All-out adversaries of state power cannot be consistent defenders of rights, for rights are an enforced uniformity, imposed by the government and funded by the public. Since the existence and protection of rights depend so directly on a healthy and vigorous state, if we want to be pro-rights we have to be pro-government to some extent as well. Without the power and authority of a well-financed state, rights are worthless.

DISMISSED AS IRRELEVANT

Today's article is my apology to my children and my grandchildren for leaving them a dysfunctional world that will make them all have a less affluent lifestyle in their old age than I have had in my senior years. One looks at the state of affairs all across the globe and realizes that the 1% has defeated the 99% and made us all slaves to their greed. Although the most obscene gap between the rich and the poor exists in the USA, our beloved Canada is not immune to the insidious evil of an economic system where all the wealth flows to those at the top.

Throughout my life, I have always strived to live frugally, because I wanted to make sure I had enough assets in old age to survive in an economic system that at its core has no compassion. I had the misfortune of being born in a country where greed is hailed as an enviable trait, and now, those who demand equality of economic opportunity are chided as envious. It is class warfare when those at the bottom beg for some economic equality, but it is not class warfare for those at the top to garner an ever larger share of the wealth while relegating the rest of us to worship at their altar of greed.

Oddly, a large number of those made slaves to the 1% actually have been brainwashed into believing that their interests are best served by allowing this gross inequity to continue, because they, too, may some day be part of the 1%. They have been hoodwinked by religious subterfuge and patriotic babble to believe that the USA offers all people equal opportunity to succeed. Even as a young child in a small North Carolina town, I could see that those at the top of the socio-economic scale always seemed to get more opportunities than those of us who lived on "the other side of the tracks."

Despite living on "the other side of the tracks," and being what would euphemistically be called "poor white trash," I watched my dad claw his way out of poverty and achieve a modicum of success as a businessman. Yet, because of our background, we were never considered the equal of the "old moneyed" classes that paraded around in their expensive clothes, luxury cars and dined at the country club. Mitt Romney likes to brag about how he did not inherit his money, but earned it on his own. That is kind of like George Bush attacking affirmative action, but not being bothered by his preferential treatment for admissions to Yale, because his dad was a graduate of the school. Romney's dad being CEO of American Motors, his childhood in the affluent Detroit suburb of Bloomfield Hills, his sojourns at exclusive private boarding schools and having parents able to afford an Ivy League education obviously did not give him an advantage over the child born to minimum wage earners in the slums of downtown Detroit. I suppose the financial assistance his dad provided when he was starting out in business did not give him a leg-up in life either. Get real! That sounds a lot like Donald Trump, who also made it on his own, even though his dad was worth 200 million dollars when Donald started in his real estate business.

Do I begrudge the rich their money? Yes, I do. I make no apologies for envying them. Why shouldn't I envy them? Most of them are born with advantages the majority of us can not even dream of in a world that makes slaves out of the 99% of us who serve the masters who control our lives. They own the places where we work. They own the companies that make our transportation. They own the mortgage companies that we are in hock to, so we can have a roof over our heads. They own the companies that supply the electricity that keeps us out of the darkness. They own the gas companies that keep us warm on cold winter nights. They own the grocery stores where we buy our food. Oh, and above all, they own the politicians whom we elect to represent us.

There was a time after World War II when the pendulum actually swung the working man's way for a brief time in the USA. Unions made it possible for people to actually be part of a growing middle class. However, Ronald Reagan brought all that to an end in 1981, when he declared war on the unions in America, and Margaret Thatcher soon followed his lead in the United Kingdom. Since then, the USA middle class has continued to contract, and the tax structure has been skewed to serve those at the top, while placing all the burdens of society on the middle class.

Let me illustrate for you how most of us fall prey to the idea that the path to happiness is through the accumulation of material things. All my life I was taught the value of a dollar, because I had two parents who survived the Great Depression. I learned from an early age that those who do not plan for the future may well wind up destitute in old age as a result of an economic system that shows no mercy. I was very fortunate as a child. Although I can vaguely remember poverty for a few of my early years, for the most part, due to my dad's business successes, my childhood was one of modest affluence. I say modest, because my father never saw the need to flaunt his affluence with fancy cars, luxurious homes or any of other the trappings of wealth.

As I got older, people often looked at me quizzically, because I was so cheap. When my three children were small, they could not understand why when I bought them hamburgers and French fries at McDonalds, I always took in a six pack of coke for them to drink. That may seem like a minor thing, but at the then price if $1.00 each, I figure that one act of frugality has probably saved me over $5,000, and my wife and I continue to do that in order to avoid the $2.50 to $3.00 charge now imposed for sodas at most restaurants with table service. Granted, I no longer take in a soda, but rather a package of Crystal Light. I just love it when they stand and watch me sprinkle my crystals into a glass of water. One restaurant manager even said, "I can't allow you to bring flavour for your water in here." My reply, "you just sold me a $10 dinner. I will not come back again, if I have to pay for a soda. I eat here once a week, so you have just cost yourself $520." He looked at me, smiled and said, "I never looked at it that way. Enjoy your meal."

Additionally, I have never owned a cell phone, so I have saved about $40 a month the last twenty years, or around $10,000. It is getting more difficult to find a pay phone, but they are available. I had satellite television that started out at $35 a month when we first arrived in Canada, but within 8 years had gone up to $90 a month for 450 channels of junk like *American Idol* and *Friends*. Realizing that we could find quality entertainment like Jack Benny, Jackie Gleason, Ozzie and Harriet, Playhouse 90 and the latest foreign films on-line, we decided television of any kind was no longer necessary. We have been television free for almost one year now and never intend on having one again.

Before I owned a new automobile, I was 57 years old, because I saw new cars as a ludicrous waste of money since they lost about 40% of their value when driven off the lot. I generally drove junk myself, while purchasing my wife a car that was two or three years old, because I knew she felt better and safer driving a newer car. In the late 1980's, I had a 1964 Ford station wagon that looked like it had been in a battle with a thrashing machine and lost. It did not bother me in the least bit to boldly drive up to the prestigious university where I was an associate professor and proudly get out of my car in a lot filled with Porsches, BMW's, Mercedes and even an occasional Rolls Royce as one of my students had a father who was a Los Angeles Rolls Royce and Ferrari dealer. Of course, my children were often embarrassed for me to drop them off at school in a car that had rusted fenders and belched out smoke from an engine that had long ago passed the amount of kilometres that would have put most cars in the junk yard.

I fondly recall my daughter one day asking me to drop her off around the corner so her friends would not see the pile of junk that she was getting out of in front of the school. Looking at the Mercedes, Lincolns and Cadillac's pulling up, I told her she should get out with pride, because her dad's car was paid for, and most of the other parents were making payments on their automobiles. Now, I realize that was too much for a middle school student to comprehend, but it is a perfect example of how we are all conditioned from an early age to worry about what other people think, so that we will buy products and services that we do not need. I, for one, have never cared what other people thought about me. I always assumed that while others were buying expensive clothes, high-priced home furnishings, fancy cars, boats, recreational vehicles and dining in fine restaurants, I was putting money away so that if I lived to be an old man, I would not be a burden on the state or my family.

MUSINGS FROM THE EDGE: A COMPENDIUM
OF THAT WHICH AFFLICTS THE HUMAN SPIRIT

I figure, at a minimum, my frugality over the years has put an additional $200,000 in my pocket. Granted, in today's world, $200,000 is chump change. At today's interest rates, even if you had 2 million dollars, your interest income would only be about $40,000 a year. Once again, only the super wealthy can truly afford to invest and reap huge rewards. I thought I had life made until the first Bush recession of 2002 took me for an $80,000 hit in the stock market. Unfortunately, that was small potatoes compared to what happened to my investments when Bush's mismanagement of the economy brought the USA to the brink of a depression in 2007. Meanwhile, he is drawing a $200,000 pension from the U.S. government and is provided with grandiose and parsimonious benefits like free healthcare the rest of his life in a nation where healthcare for most people is a privilege rather than a right. Ironically, he doesn't even need the income or benefits as his grandfather, Prescott Bush, who made a fabulous fortune trading with the Nazis, provided trust funds for his children and grandchildren. Yet, the very people who are abused by this system, often line up to cheer and aggrandize these scions of privilege.

I was shocked by the large number of Canadians who turned out to cheer those royal parasites right after their marriage in a grandiose and ostentatious ceremony. How ironic that people actually want to drop to their knees before those who look at the great unwashed masses with disdain and contempt. Fortunately, when they showed up in Quebec, they were greeted with boos by people who are tired of footing the bill for the royal leeches to visit a country where 68% of the people want to completely cut ties with an outdated and completely useless monarchy.

MUSINGS FROM THE EDGE: A COMPENDIUM OF THAT WHICH AFFLICTS THE HUMAN SPIRIT

In 2000, after the appointment of George Bush as President in the USA, I began to see the handwriting on the wall that would finally lead to the complete destruction of any semblance of fairness in a society devoted to the enslavement of all humanity to the culture of greed. I was making an incredible salary for doing an easy job I loved, but at 57, I took about an 80% cut in pay to escape the misery of a life in a fascist state.

Today, I still live my intensely frugal lifestyle in a country with a social safety net that makes me proud to be Canadian. Yet, as I watch my assets diminish because most of my retirement income is derived from the USA, I cannot help but fret for my children and grandchildren, even the ones lucky enough to call Canada home, as the corporate theocracy's insidious reach will destroy everything in its march to enslave all of humanity to the bottom line. The world has been turned over to the rich and powerful, and those of us in the 99% have been dismissed as irrelevant.

A LOUSY FREE T-SHIRT

As usual, the sports fanatics are fawning all over the sentimental story of Kevin Ware's broken leg and how his team rallied for a victory over Duke. That is one reason I stopped watching television years ago, chucking my 365 channels of junk for the freedom to use my brains rather than let manipulative corporations brainwash me into contributing to the society of greed that puts a price tag on everything from the Sunday morning collection plates in church that are selling Jesus to Little League Baseball that is now charging $1.00 to $5.00 in some places for the parents to see their future multimillionaire sports icons hit a ball and make great fielding plays to prove their worth to society.

The ridiculous sentimentality of the classic story of an injured player inspiring his shaken team to victory has been around since that icon of stupidity and worshiper of the privileged, Ronald Reagan, a mediocre actor and equally mediocre President., played the Gipper in a movie that has promulgated an incident that actually never occurred as the truth to impressionable people who believe if it is in a movie, it must be true.

Now, we have reached the point where tragedy becomes farce. Adidas, seeing dollar signs from the terrible incident that occurred on the court in conjunction with the University of Louisville that, no doubt, teaches courses in ethics, decided to sell a $1.00 T-shirt for $24.95 with Kevin Ware's number 5 on it and the words "Rise to the Occasion" scrawled across the back.

So, you have a non-profit institution that pays its coach nearly 5 million dollars a year, while probably laying-off non-tenured professors because of budget problems, whose million dollar a year president approves an outlandish money crab by playing on the sentimentality of impressionable children and adult morons who are swept up in the splendor of the iconic sports moment when tragedy brings triumph. What garbage! What kind of institution, corporation and association for athletics would see a tibia snap through a 20-year-old's skin on national television and figure out the financial potential from such a horrendous accident. Meanwhile, not one dime of that money would ever get to the injured player, because he is an amateur. Again, what garbage!

MUSINGS FROM THE EDGE: A COMPENDIUM
OF THAT WHICH AFFLICTS THE HUMAN SPIRIT

This may be the end of this young man's career, and he will get nothing but a pat on the back and be sent off into the wilderness inhabited by all those athletes who are used and then discarded by the NCAA and the institutions that make millions off their labour. Furthermore, he can lose his scholarship since he can no longer play, and in a nation where healthcare is a privilege rather than a right, his family may have to come up some of the money needed for his rehabilitation, as there is a limit on the insurance coverage in a country where the hospitals are just as greedy as the University of Louisville, the NCAA and Adidas. Going forward, no one can guess what might happen in terms of medical expenses. If Kevin has lifelong medical bills associated with his injury, he could be squarely responsible for the cost. These are things that are not guaranteed to players that are injured, and no matter how hard it might be for people to understand, that is the truth in a nation that has greed at the very core of its character.

Universities are corporations, and now-a-days most presidents of universities are corporate executives and sports are nothing but products they brazenly sell while maintaining the façade that the players are students first and athletes second. In the case of Kevin, their brazen money grab caused outrage, so the three parties to this scam backed off and will donate the money to various charities. Hey, the charities they will be donating to probably have million dollars a year executives simply running another scam. What does Ware get out of all this bowing before the altar of greed? Hey, maybe they will give him a lousy free T-shirt.

CAPITALISM'S FAILURE

J. Wayne Frye

MUSINGS FROM THE EDGE: A COMPENDIUM
OF THAT WHICH AFFLICTS THE HUMAN SPIRIT

America's financial system is on the verge of collapse. The house of cards that was started by Ronald Reagan with his insane tax cuts for the wealthy and corporations in 1981, and was brought to its apex under the leadership of the most inarticulate, idiotic buffoon to every step into the White House, George Bush, has come tumbling down. While the speculators and banks on Wall Street, that are the champions of free enterprise, come to the government with out-stretched hands, once again, the average guy who is told socialism is an abomination, will be expected to bail-out these bastions of commerce who have gorged themselves at the trough of governmental largesse for far too long.

Although not technically possible, George Bush has seen to it that he will actually be getting a third, fourth, fifth, sixth and seventh term. Why? Because it will require at least one generation (20 years) to correct the mess he has left for his predecessors to clean up. His insane policies will delay America being able to offer its citizens what every other civilized country in the world offers – free health care. Furthermore, his incompetence will delay improvements in education, veterans benefits, social security, infrastructure and a host of social programs. I suppose one should simply shrug his or her shoulders and say that this is what Americans deserve for electing this buffoon to two terms in the White House. (Well, actually electing him once, as he was appointed by the Supreme Court the first time.) Unfortunately, there are about 48% of Americans who were smart enough to say "no" to this cocky, swaggering cowboy politician who never saw a corporation he did not love. They will be suffering along with those who fell for the fear-mongering, flag-waving, patriotic and religious babble

J. Wayne Frye   63

that pours out of Republicans like water over Niagara Falls.

The people of America and the world will be paying for this man-made economic disaster for years to come through higher prices for food, gas and a variety of necessities. The foreclosures, evictions, unemployment, increasing poverty and turmoil will all be fostered by this economic melt-down precipitated at 1600 Pennsylvania Avenue by a bunch of self-righteous, arrogant Fascists who turned the American economy over to a pack of thieves who look on the American treasury as their petty cash drawer. To top it all off, when Obama came into office, he refused to prosecute these thieves.

Ultimately, the blame will be placed on Americans living beyond their means. No doubt, most Americans do live far beyond their means as a result of marketing that convinces them happiness can only be bought by purchasing things. Just look in the typical driveway of a middle class family where you will see two new cars, maybe a boat or recreational vehicle and a nicely manicured lawn in front of a home with huge monthly payments that requires both parents to work so they can buy their kids the latest $200 sneakers, cell-phones and name-brand clothes and accessories. Maybe we should blame them for falling for the Madison Avenue hype that tells them that happiness can only be measured by the things you have. Wall Street makes credit easily available, so Americans can "buy all this happiness," and most Americans fall for it hook, line and sinker. Wall Street and Madison Avenue see the average American as nothing more than a consumer begging to be fleeced. Yet, are we supposed to hold those who manipulate the vast un-thinking masses blameless? This crisis was not caused by the easily manipulated consumers buying things they did not need and could not afford. It was caused by an irrational free-market system and the insatiable greed of a small class of economic barons who do not know the meaning of "enough." Why do those who have the most always think they must have more?

The whole economic meltdown is just one more indictment of the capitalist system that is based on the idea that you can not have a moneyed class unless you have an exploited class.

CONFISCATE THE WEALTH

Free speech does not exist in a world where corporations own the airwaves. Is my right to free speech equal to that of Rupert Murdoch, who owns a multibillion-dollar media empire? Moreover, a large part of the state apparatus, the military and the state bureaucracy, is not subject to elections.

The voting population does not make decisions like whether or not to go to war. Workers have no democratic say-so over the most basic economic decisions that affect their lives. We can't fire our bosses or vote to change working conditions. Even today, every freedom granted to us is hemmed in by political and economic qualifications. In many states in the USA, for example, public workers are denied the right to strike. That is why, in spite of people's right to vote, they are forced to engage in demonstrations and strikes that are outside the formal political process. There is class warfare in America, but it is the middle class against their fellow middle classes and the poor. Wisconsin governor Scott Walker, as a representative of the Koch brothers - not the people of Wisconsin, has dismantled state worker's right to strike, which is supported by over 50% of the population who are jealous of state workers' salaries, pensions and benefits. Rather than feeding their jealousy of the working classes who have the sense to unionize, why don't they unionize themselves and force their corporate bosses to give them salaries and benefits equal to that of the unionized state workers? No, they had rather make villains out of those who have the courage to unionize and demand fair treatment in their workplace than get off their knees and do something about their own plight.

Parliamentary democracy, like that in Canada, has been fairly successful in providing the illusion of real democracy in a society where a small number of very wealthy people and the bureaucrats who serve them make all the important decisions. But there are times when even formal democracy becomes too threatening to the powers that be, as the many coups around the world show. As the German revolutionary Rosa Luxemburg pointed out at the turn of the 19th century: "In this society, the representative institutions, democratic in form, are in content the instruments of the interests of the ruling class." This manifests itself in a tangible fashion in the fact that as soon as democracy shows the tendency to negate its class character and become transformed into an instrument of the real interests of the population, the democratic forms are sacrificed by the bourgeoisie, and by its state representatives. This is a pattern that has been consistent throughout history.

Until the whole system of capitalism is totally destroyed and the immense wealth of the 1% confiscated, there will never be any freedom for those of us in the 99%.

GREED

In a world where one's worth is judged by the things he or she possess, is it any wonder that people go crazy over the opportunity to save $50 on a big-screen television? After all, you are worthless without that magnificent magic box that provides you with such stellar entertainment as *American Idol* or the latest exploits of those media whores, the *Kardashians*. As a person who has not owned a television for many years, I can certainly attest to the absolute fact that life is much better and incredibly more fulfilling without that box of banality that wastes so much of people's valuable time. However, I do understand why people need it. Hey, if you didn't have television, you might have to read a book. Who would want to do that?

Greed is like a plague that spreads rapidly across the land, consuming all in its path. So, as I sat at home, avoiding all the Black Friday and Cyber Monday madness, I realize that there is one evil in the world that is at the heart of why there is so little compassion. Oh, if I believed in God, I would ask him to save the world from this malady that runs like a raging river rising above its banks and destroys everything in its path. Yes, I would plead for an end to the greatest evil of all – greed and the capitalist system that feeds it.

THE RICH THEY REPRESENT

One of the most pernicious and utterly inane economic falsehoods you will hear from those rich loving

Republicans in the United States of America is that high taxes will stifle growth. By this view, if taxes on the wealthy are raised the economy can't grow as fast.

That is an argument that has been disproved time and time again. Yet, the Republicans refuse to look at the facts, because they simply refuse to make the rich pay their fair share. Taxes were far higher on top incomes in the three decades after World War II than they have been since. Yes, we all know that the 91% rate was only paid by a hand full of immensely rich people, but the point it that it was paid by some, and the income disparity in those days was nowhere as obscene as it is today as the distribution of income was far more equal thinks to a highly unionized working class. Yet, the American economy grew faster in those years than it has grown since tax rates were slashed in 1981 by the greatest union buster who ever sat in the White House. Of course, who was voted the greatest American – Ronald Reagan.

This wasn't a post-war aberration. Bill Clinton raised taxes on the wealthy in the 1990's, and the economy produced faster job growth and higher wages than it did after George W. Bush slashed taxes on the rich in his first term. If you need more evidence, consider modern Germany, where taxes on the wealthy are much higher than they are in the USA and the distribution of income is far more equal. But Germany's average annual growth has been greater than that in the United States.

You see, higher taxes on the wealthy can finance more investments in infrastructure and education, which are vital for growth and the economic prospects of the middle class. Higher taxes on the wealthy also allow for lower taxes on the middle income earners, potentially restoring enough middle class purchasing power to keep the economy humming along. As has happened in recent years, when disposable income is concentrated at the top, the middle class doesn't have enough money to boost the economy.

What should have been learned over the last half century is that growth doesn't trickle down from the top, despite what Ronald Reagan said. A rising tide does not lift all boats into a sea of plenty. It dashes many boats onto the rocks. Real growth percolates upward from working people who are adequately educated, sufficiently rewarded, and who feel they have a fair chance to make it. Fairness is not incompatible with growth. It is an absolute necessity for it, but don't expect the Republicans to ever give up their commitment to the rich, regardless of what the truth is. Truth has no place in an economic system based on greed.

THE SILVER SPOON SYNDROME

I was asked to write this column, because I was told that I was a person who knew how to be frugal and make it pay off. Well, I will not go into detail, but suffice it to say that recent events in my life indicate my frugality will pay off for others more than it will pay off for me. However, since it will be used to benefit the ones I love, I am satisfied to a certain degree, as I have always gotten more satisfaction from giving thsn receiving.

At my age, I often look back on my life and ask why I did certain things. My goal was to always take care of those whom I loved. My children were central to my young adulthood and I doted on them, because they gave me the childhood I never had as a result of family circumstances that often necessitated that I be the adult when I was a child.

The world is filled with people who live for the moment with no concern for the future. They think that weekly pay cheque will always be there, and that somehow, magically an all-benevolent government will mail them an old age pension that is actually large enough to live on. For that reason, over 90% of the people who retire simply do not have the funds and annuities necessary to maintain any semblance of the lifestyle they lived before retirement. Buying $200 sneakers, name brand clothes, taking expensive vacations, spending large sums for cable television that does nothing but provide pabulum for 12 year old minds, purchasing items that boost ego rather than satisfy a real need are foolish manifestations of those who have let their minds be massaged by the corporations that imprison them in an ever growing spiral of searching for the good life that they think can only be attained through conspicuous consumption. Without these material items, people think their lives are somehow less than they should be. For those smart enough to battle against this insidiousness, I offer the following advice:

1. Never depend on a single income source. Always have backups to assure economic security. I am constantly doing this without anyone even being aware of what I am doing. There is no need to broadcast what you are trying to accomplish. Some things are better left unsaid, as I can attest to since I have put my foot in my mouth more than once.

MUSINGS FROM THE EDGE: A COMPENDIUM
OF THAT WHICH AFFLICTS THE HUMAN SPIRIT

2. If you buy things you do not need or things that come with a designer label, you will soon have to sell things that you do need to pay for those that you do not need.

3. Do not save what is left after spending, but spend what is left after saving. I always doubled what was taken out of my income for retirement, because I felt it was important to force myself to save, rather than depend on having enough sense to always put a little aside.

4. Never test the depth of river with both feet. Always keep one foot on shore for safety. The sea of life is filled with sharks, so always be leery.

5. Do not put all your eggs in one basket. Unless you have a government pension, do not expect a corporation funded pension to be there. Corporations and oft times the pension plans they fund go bankrupt. Why do you think the executives all have separately funded guaranteed pension plans? They want no part of a pension plan that is tied to the fate of the corporation that they may someday bankrupt for personal gain. And just because you have a union, unless it is a government guaranteed pension, do not expect it to secure your future. Unions are really nothing but corporations themselves with high paid executives who have little in common with the people they are supposed to represent. So, even the organization that organization is corrupted by greed.

6. Security is expensive in terms of self-denial. Most people are unwilling to deny themselves immediate gratification for delayed gratification. Every day I see those with little trying to live like they have a lot. Don't make the mistake of thinking tomorrow will mean an

increase in income. I know from experience working with the Los Angeles Unified School District that employees are sometimes asked to take a pay cut to keep the company afloat. Asked the unionized workers at GM, Ford and Chrysler how many times they have been forced to take a pay cut to keep their jobs.

So, what is the bottom line? Simply that those not born with a silver spoon in their mouths need to stop living like they were. Only a select few in capitalism get a free ride to the top, and most of us aren't that lucky. Be eternally vigilant, because in a system based on greed, there are always those who want to steal what you worked hard for in order to put more money in their own already stuffed pockets. Remember that in capitalism there must always be more losers than winners. Most of us simply will always be on the outside looking in, so be eternally vigilant.

This has only been a cursory exploration of how a mountain of lies is used to keep people in economic bondage. With the fall of the Soviet Union, the entire world now must bow before American economic blackmail. Even China has turned its economy over to the elitists. It has the fastest growing number of billionaires in the world now, and the fortunes of these people, like the American elite is built on the backs of working men and women.

CHAPTER 3

HOW TO STAND AGAINST A SYSTEM
BASED ON GREED

I left the USA to escape the growing fascism and the constant coddling of the rich and privileged who have been allowed to buy the government lock, stock and barrel as a result of the conservative controlled Supreme Court siding with corporations over the people. Watching the USA meddle in the Canadian election, which saw a conservative seize power with only about 35% of the vote, reminded me that there is no place safe from the American terrorism that subverts the economic and political well-being of most people in the world. Only Cuba and a few equally radical Muslin fascists still stand against the might of a nation that wants to make slaves of all working men and women, so that corporations can ride the wave of exploitation into a harbour of splendorous luxury for the 1% who think they are entitled. I share here some pleas for sanity in a world that is an asylum of economic lunacy, and the truth is that the inmates (the rich) are running the asylum and putting a straight jacket of poverty on far too many.

MUSINGS FROM THE EDGE: A COMPENDIUM
OF THAT WHICH AFFLICTS THE HUMAN SPIRIT

A SYSTEM THAT SEEKS TO ENSLAVE THEM

Let me attempt to explain how the economic melt-down caused by the USA and the wanna-be cowboy from Texas literally destroyed the lives of countless millions of older people all over the entire world, who thought they were going to enjoy a retirement that they had worked so hard to earn.

A few years ago, I decided to immigrate to Canada in search of a more just and humane society in order to free myself from the fascism taking hold south of us. Getting $1.51 for every U.S. dollar I brought into Canada, I deduced that I could have a nice, but not lavish, retirement in a country where healthcare was a right rather than a privilege, where the rich were not afforded unfair tax-breaks, where protecting the social safety net was considered the duty of a government that served the people rather than special interests and where bombs and bullets were not used as a tool to force other countries into submission. For a few short years, I thought I was rich. Then, George Bush's insane military adventures, economic incompetence and coddling of the corporations and wealthy, brought my economic security to a halt as I watched my monthly U.S. retirement checks dwindle down to as low as 91 cents Canadian to the U.S. dollar. Meanwhile, my savings were trapped in banks that were only willing to pay 1% interest while inflation soared at an official 3%, but, was in fact, more likely between 8% to 10%. It does not take a mathematical genius to figure out that my economic viability has been seriously threatened. Meanwhile, the jerk that set all this in motion is drawing a huge U.S. government pension and laughing all the way to the bank. Additionally, the disappointing, spineless coward who replaced him does noting but acquiesce to the demands of the Republican Party that continues to believe in trickle down economics that allows we peons to fight for scraps from the table of plenty reserved for their corporate and wealthy benefactors.

I have the good fortune to be a Canadian citizen, so I know that I will not go without healthcare, shelter and something to eat. However, I spent my life scrimping and saving so I could accumulate a nest egg for my old age, and hopefully accumulate a little something to leave my children. However, in a world based on greed, the barons of capitalism have been allowed to rape, pillage and plunder those of us with moderate means. I actually consider myself fortunate, because I do have a few assets and a dollar or two left to last me for the few years I have remaining. However, for those with more modest means, I fear that the world is going to be increasingly divided into the haves and have-nots. The days of serfdom are returning with a vengeance, and the serfs are too complacent and demoralized to rise up in rebellion against a system that seeks to enslave them.

IT IS BETTER TO DIE STANDING THAN TO LIVE ON YOUR KNEES

Thanks to the malfeasance of George Bush, the world economy was put in its worst crisis since the 1930's ion 2007. This is the man who took a budget surplus and turned it into a disastrous deficit. He is also the man who touted the private insurance industry as the reason America has the best healthcare system in the world. (In truth it actually ranks 37th.) Of course, he forgot to say it was the greatest only if you were wealthy enough to afford the very best insurance money could buy. And he has the very best insurance money can buy, as it is furnished to him courtesy of the government which he and the rest of the heartless Republican politicians say should stay out of healthcare – well, stay out when it comes to the average Joe, but not when it comes to the politicians who give themselves the best retirement package and the best healthcare that the government can provide. To the Republicans, government is only bad when it is helping the average Joe, but when it hands welfare to the rich and powerful it is doing the people's business in a fair and equitable way.

U.S. banks and corporations sat on a record $2 trillion in cash while watching the economy tank with their only concern their own welfare.. In most sectors, profits returned, often to record levels and tax rates for corporations and wealthy individuals remained at historic lows during the administration of a Democrat who promised to make the rich pay their fair share. Of course, he has said that he will not cave-in this time. Yeah, like he isn't going to once again bend to the rich-loving Republicans who are more loyal to Grover Norquist's mantra of no tax increases than they are to the country they are supposed to love.

Welcome to 21st-century capitalism, a topsy-turvy world in which poverty for many and unimaginable wealth for a tiny few stand side by side. But unlike earlier times, when slave and feudal societies weren't efficient enough to adequately feed, clothe and house everyone, today's crisis laden economy is caused by all the wealth being concentrated in too few hands. If properly managed, there is enough wealth in the world to feed, cloth and house every human being. However, as long as corporate capitalism exists, this will never happen, because that would lift too many people out of slavery to the few whose unquenchable greed for more and more will never be satisfied.

The technological innovations that made capitalism's incredible productivity possible could permanently free humanity from the scourge of poverty, want and hunger. Of course, the very nature of capitalism makes this an impossibility, because greed, according to the American thought process, is actually good. Greed is a great motivator. Sure, it motivates people to enslave workers so they can produce wealth for the 1%. The problem with capitalism is that how much is produced is not decided on the basis of what people need to survive. It is based on what will return a maximum profit for the owners of offices, factories and construction sites. If there is too much to be sold profitably, the greater efficiency of new production techniques has the effect of leading to layoffs and demands for worker concessions, instead of a lighter workload and a higher standard of living for the people who are actually doing the work. So, in today's world, a corporation that does well sees no need to reward the workers that made this possible. Rather, it wants to demand more and more of them.

The mere fact that 20% of the world's population does not have enough to eat is a damning indictment of capitalism's obsession with profits over people. A truly socialist society would not be concerned with profits but with the needs of the people. In place of the destructive dynamic of free market competition, a socialist economy would be planned to make sure there were surpluses of food, clothing, health care and shelter before turning to the production of luxury goods that only a minority of people can afford. I know it would pain people like Mitt Romney to have to give up one of his wife's Cadillac's, but in a socialist society maybe a starving child in the ghettos that dot America might actually be considered more important than the constant stroking of a rich woman's ego. Maybe she would be forced to get by on one Cadillac. I know it would be tough, but surely she could survive.

Apologists for capitalism insist that socialist planning can not work. They say that any attempt to plan such a complex and large economy would be inefficient. They love to use examples like the former Soviet Union, which was not a socialized economy by any sane definition of the term. Stalinism in Russia was the result of the failure of socialist revolution to spread when he hijacked the state for personal aggrandizement, not the inevitable consequence of planning. The isolation of the Russian Revolution meant that the relatively backward economy of the USSR had to ruthlessly exploit its working class in order to carry out industrialization and compete militarily with western capitalism which actually spent itself into bankruptcy for fear that socialism might supplant capitalism if workers began to realize that they were in bondage to the capitalist class. In other words, the Soviet Union lacked what Frederick Engels and Karl Marx described as a prerequisite for a socialist society, the willingness to always be in a constant state of revolution against those who were in power. Revolution does not happen and then stop. It is a never-ending process.

J. Wayne Frye

MUSINGS FROM THE EDGE: A COMPENDIUM
OF THAT WHICH AFFLICTS THE HUMAN SPIRIT

The real problem the capitalist has with socialism is that they realize the people who really do the work would actually be in control of their own destiny under socialism. And here is the decisive point: as soon as human labor realizes without them there is no capitalist class, they will see that there overloads are no longer necessary. Can you imagine what it would be like to see the George Bush's, The Rockefellers, The Waltons, the Kock brothers, the Mitt Romney's and the Donald Trump's of the world have to actually put in a day's work on the factory floor?

Of course, simply posing the desirability of a democratically planned socialist society is not sufficient to make this change occur. The capitalist class will not hand over control of the economy just because a socialist economy is far more rational than capitalism. They will fight furiously to maintain their power, and they have at their disposal the politicians, the governments, the police and a world of easily manipulated workers who are too timid and fearful to make a stand against their oppressors. In this writer's humble opinion, this change can probably not take place peacefully, because the capitalist will never give up his position of power willingly. I am a product of the 60's, and I still long for the day when that old phrase, "all power to the people," will become a realty rather than just an empty phrase shouted by those of us who once saw an opportunity for real change slip from our grasp. Each person must face the indignity of corporate slavery by realizing that it is better to die standing than to live on your knees. Unfortunately, complacency and loss of hope will continue to keep most people on their knees.

PATRITOIC NONSENSE

MUSINGS FROM THE EDGE: A COMPENDIUM
OF THAT WHICH AFFLICTS THE HUMAN SPIRIT

I have never understood the incredibly exaggerated public respect that is accorded to professional soldiers. Notice the word professional. They elected to do the job. They were not drafted like I was. Granted, those who enlist are generally from the lower socio-economic class, so they often do it, because, unlike the 1%, they have to defend the rights of people like Mitt Romney to give their sons 20 million dollars each. Do you think Mitt Romney or his sons ever even entertained the thought of defending freedom by enlisting in the army to defend the country they love so much. Hey, even that old slacker George Bush joined the National Guard. Granted, afte5r his father got a guaranteed that he would never have to serve in combat, but at least he signed up, so he could have some good buddies to go drinking with.

Barrack Obama is always extolling the virtues of the military just like his war-loving opponents in the Republican party. Just like them, he sees the need to defend the rights of the oil companies, so he has no problems sending the poor to die for oil.

Why do we owe these soldiers respect? How many innocent women and children do they slaughter in the name of liberty? Yet, we make heroes out of them. Even Obama calls John McCain a great hero. How heroic is it to drop bombs on women and children from 80,000 feet? The 9/11 hijackers were much more heroic, as they knowingly sacrificed their lives. Meanwhile, McCain, being the son of an Admiral, got preferential treatment as a POW. And what of firefighters and police who are always proclaimed heroes. If doing your job makes you a hero, every American who gets up and goes to work daily is a hero. I served in that utterly insane enterprise called the Vietnam War. Does that make me a hero? I don't think so. The real heroes were my fellow Americans who had the courage to say "no" and fled to Canada rather than serve in an immoral and illegal war.

Soldiers do not deserve the exaggerated respect they receive. Soldiers join the army knowing full well that they will have to kill people. I cannot begin to imagine the mind-set of someone who thinks this is ok. The fact that these men and women are apparently okay with the idea of being paid to kill others is pretty disturbing to say the least and hardly worthy of respect. Frankly, I find it contemptible to congratulate those who kill for a living. Now your trenchant flag-waver will defend these soldiers by saying that they are defending their country but that is not true. US soldiers are involved in wars which have little or no bearing on the security of their country. Sure, there are important geo-strategic interests at stake, but it is not the case that there is a massive risk to the ordinary citizens of the USA from Islamic extremists, let alone Afghans or Iraqis. Look at the economic factors and any idiot could comprehend that the real purpose of U.S. wars is corporate enrichment.

There are plenty of people who do far more important jobs in our societies but receive far less credit. Just off the top of my head it should be fairly obvious that, for a country not threatened by war - doctors, nurses, teachers, social workers, all perform far more useful jobs than soldiers whose job it is to kill. I don't think we should put these guys up on a pedestal either as there are plenty of reasons why people choose these jobs, not all of them gratifying, but the fact is that they contribute vastly more to society than a man with a gun in his hand.

All of these groups, especially teachers and social workers, are subject to all kinds of abuse from the media and other commentators when things don't go perfectly. Yet it seems as though soldiers can do no wrong, unless of course they are actually implicated in a war crime, in which case these soldiers are hastily labelled as 'not representative' of the rest of the army. The fact is that they are representative. I often visit Victoria, British Columbia which is 45 minutes south of my home, and I am always appalled when a United States ship is in port, because the place is filled with swaggering, arrogant, bombastic American military personnel walking about as if they are Gods to be feared and worshipped.

THAT LITTLE VILLAGE BENEATH THE SNOW-COVERED MESA

The sky above is obliterated by white, fluffy, mist-filled fog that seems to descend from the heavens and embrace the snow-covered ground upon which I glide effortlessly on my snowmobile. I am on the way to an isolated aboriginal community heading across only make-shift trails leading to those few people who still live the way their forefathers did. They are free of the trappings of modern society, some even living without electricity or the ever present satellite television dish. The cell-phone I borrowed only works sporadically, as the signal is often blocked by atmospheric or terrain conditions. Out here in the wilderness, I am at the mercy of the elements and the skill of my snowmobile driver who seems to effortlessly navigate through the landscape, as he constantly reminds me to keep an eye on the slid filled with medical supplies we are pulling behind us. This is not a job for the faint-at-heart, but it is a job the driver clasps to with great zeal, since it affords him an opportunity to connect with his heritage. He is one of those aboriginals who was born in the city, but later in life, realized that he was a descendant of a noble race of people who had their land stolen and their way of life destroyed by people who considered them savages. To pay homage to his people, he decided to devote his life in service to aboriginals who are shunned by a society that thinks those who live simply and eschew the ever-prevalent culture of greed are somehow irrelevant in the modern world. Turning your back on greed is a difficult task, but there are societies that have managed to do it. Of course, America is not, nor will it probably ever be one that does this, because the idea of fairness is not part of the system.

As we drive toward a tall, snow cover mesa, at its base are a row of simple log huts with smoke rising majestically out of ancient stone chimneys. Approaching them, the sounds of our whirring motor bounce off the mesa and reverberate throughout the desolate valley. Within a hundred feet of the huts, we see doors sprang open and people begin to eagerly wave. His monthly journey to this village offers more than medical help. It is a journey of discovery that affords him an opportunity to share in the lives of people who know serenity, peace and tranquility that those of us in so-called civilization can only dream about. These people do not even know it, but they are living in paradise.

The culture of greed that makes us all think that happiness comes with a price tag has no place here. These people welcome us with open arms and gladly share a warm blanket, a cozy seat by the fireplace or a caribou steak. With no need for refrigeration during the winter months, everyone hangs their food in a community storage shed, and gladly shares it with all members of the small village. Hunger or lack of shelter would simply not be tolerated in a society where the pain of one is the pain of all. This approach to life is unimaginable in the cities.

After a day of accessing the health of the villagers, as night falls, we mount our snowmobile and head back to what is euphemistically called civilization. The two hour journey will seem tedious as we leave behind a way of life that a few brave souls are fighting desperately to protect from the ever insidious spread of the corporate-based culture that makes slaves of us all. I intend to do all I can to assist in helping these noble people maintain a lifestyle that must be insulated from the cruelties of a society where everything has a price-tag.

Leaving the village far behind, the sound of the roaring engine penetrates the bitterly cold, mist-filled darkness, and I am bewildered as I see the bright lights of the city in the distance. Am I now headed back to civilization, or is the real civilization back in that little village beneath the snow covered mesa?

IN THE FACE OF DECEIT
TRUTH BECOMES REVOLUTIONARY

O.K., I know that my readers get tired of my rants against USA, but today's column will once again centre around that country I left behind in 2003, as I want to explore the rash of e-mails I received from friends, relatives and acquaintances who are appalled that the U.S. Supreme Court ruled that Obamacare is indeed constitutional. I find it particularly interesting that so many of them are contemplating moving from the country of their birth. Actually, I would encourage them to do so, because for the first time in their lives, they might find out what real freedom is like, rather than the propagandized and fear-mongered brand of democracy to which they all willingly submit as a result of brainwashing into the belief that America is the paramount democratic nation.

I would assume most of them would not consider a Third World country for their new home, so, if they were to move to Canada, any European country, Australia, or even some Third World countries, they would get the very thing they seem to find so abhorrent in their current situation: universal, free health care. Yes, it could even be called by that evil term - socialized medicine, as it is better to let a corporation control healthcare than the government in America.

Even Mexico is instituting universal, free health care in 2015. The fact is that the USA is the only First World country where health care is profit-based. That is one reason it ranks 37th in the world in quality of health care. Americans say they don't want a government bureaucrat between them and their doctor, but they are perfectly willing to let an over-compensated health care CEO make life and death decisions based on the profit motive. Health care in America is the most expensive in the world, because drug companies, HMO's and insurance companies rake 25% off the top for obscene profits. What kind of nation makes health care a privilege rather than a right? That question is one of the reasons I left the United States of America and am now a proud Canadian where freedom is practiced rather than propagandized to the uninformed.

MUSINGS FROM THE EDGE: A COMPENDIUM
OF THAT WHICH AFFLICTS THE HUMAN SPIRIT

I find it especially disconcerting that many of the irate e-mailers like to call themselves "good Christians." Do these Christians think that their beloved Jesus would sanction a system that allows to the poor and disenfranchised to be denied health care? Would Jesus sanction a system that forces people into bankruptcy to pay for health care? Do they think Jesus would support an economic system that lets all the "good things" flow to those at the top while making slaves out of the other 99%? As I said in my book, *When Jesus Came to Jersey as the Son of Thunder*, Jesus was a revolutionary who would have been more at home with Che Guevara than most ministers who stand in the pulpits of America on Sundays.

I wrote several books that have been moderate best-sellers on Amazon.com. One of them, a biography (*Worth*) of my father details how he had to spend 1.2 million dollars on my mother's illnesses, because she was denied insurance after a stroke. He worked hard all his life to accumulate some wealth, but within a few years, he saw it dissipated, because he had the misfortune to live in a country where health care was a privilege, rather than a right.

So, to my Canadian readers, I say be thankful that you live in a country where the people understand that health care is a right, not a privilege. I will leave you and the friends, acquaintances and relatives to whom I am also sending this column with the words from Jesus in my book, *When Jesus Came to Jersey as the Son of Thunder:* "Those who truly love justice will always stand with me against the evil of tyrants who wrap all of you in bondage to greed and judgemental arrogance. I have suffered mightily because in the face of deceit, truth becomes revolutionary." (*The Son of Thunder*)

GRATEFUL TO BE A CANADIAN

Thanks to a friend who sent me an e-mail containing another individual's tirade against those in America who pay no taxes, today I am going to address once again the gargantuan lies promulgated by those rich-loving Republicans south of us who have no problem providing welfare for the wealthy and corporations, but resent money going to individuals in America who pay "no taxes." Like most things that come out of Republican mouths, this is just another lie to pit the middle class against the poor, while the rich continue to laugh at the gullibility of the suckers they convince to believe that it is the 47% who are the leeches rather than the rich. The guys shouting loudest against the non-tax payers have no problem with a man like Mitt Romney, who pays around 15% in taxes on millions he earns every year, getting a free ride from the same government that takes around 30% out of the average working man's wages.

Most people in Canada, even members of the Conservative Party, get a good laugh out of watching Americans like Mitt Romney spend years running for President, when, in this country, we are smart enough to limit campaigns to approximately 38 days by law. Now, even though the American people had the good sense to turn their backs on a man who was poised to hand the rich another big tax break, the Republican "let's love the rich" machine is still in high gear trying to protect the wealthy from those evil 47% who are just freeloaders.

MUSINGS FROM THE EDGE: A COMPENDIUM
OF THAT WHICH AFFLICTS THE HUMAN SPIRIT

Let's take a look at that 47%. Most all of those people do pay social security taxes on the first approximately $108,000. Of course, most earn no where near that much. Meanwhile, those making $20,000,000 a year, like Mitt Romney, pay no social security tax after they reach the $108,000 plateau. (Talk about a regressive tax - the poorer you are, the more you pay! This is probably the most unfair tax in the world.) In addition, people in this group must pay Medicare taxes, while people like Romney, who don't take a salary, do not have to pay any Medicare taxes. And this is the man who called 47% of Americans leeches.

Of course, almost one-third of those not paying taxes are the elderly. I suppose the Republicans think those who worked all their lives should spend their old-age going through dumpsters for their food, or see if they can get an $8.00 an hour job at Wal-Mart when they are 80. (Yes Canadians, that is right, the average Wal-Mart wage in America is $8.85, unlike Canada where it is $14.65.) Incidentally, substantial numbers of this 47% subset, both among seniors and working class whites, vote consistently for Republicans. Talk about voting against your own interests. Of course, one big reason is that the Republicans love God more than the Democrats, and the working class whites are more upset about two men having sex with each other than they are about where their next meal is coming from.

Ironically, it was the Republican Presidents who made a decision to reduce the taxes on the poor. Why? Because they used that as a ploy to lower the rates on the wealthy. So, the person making $15,000 a year working at Wal-Mart got a $350 tax cut by being taken off the rolls.

Meanwhile, the person making one million dollars a year got a $165,000 tax cut. That is what Republicans call fairness.

The reason the poor don't have tax liability is that the country made a decision, under Republican Presidents, to reduce the tax burden on the poor. More specifically, Republican Presidents made that decision to compensate for the fact that they wanted to give rich people a giant tax cut. So they made them "broad-based" to make them look somewhat more equitable. When you look at graphs of the percent of Americans who don't pay income taxes, you see huge jumps after Ronald Reagan's 1986 tax reform and George W. Bush's 2001 and 2003 tax cuts. So whenever you hear that half of Americans don't pay federal income taxes, remember that Ronald Reagan and George W. Bush were the chief culprits. They are also two of the worst Presidents in history when it comes to deficits. Like FDR, Clinton and Obama got stuck with messes created by Republicans who are still determined to this day to dismantle the New Deal and go back to a feudal society where the middle class and poor will serve the lords of the manor.

So, it was the Republicans who created a "nation of so-called moochers" that could immediately be pointed to by Republican politicians, to divide the lower classes and separate them. The middle class, which has some understanding that they pay taxes, will envy those who do not, and look to the very Republicans that made this happen to rectify the situation. It serves class and racial politics to have this large underclass that "doesn't" pay taxes. Conservative politicians point to the "takers" and say that they want to hike taxes on the rich out of envy and frustration. They say that if those people don't pay taxes they don't deserve services from the federal government. So there are multiple ways that creating this ridiculous 47% myth serves conservative theories of government.

Frankly, I was shocked that a slim majority of Americans did not fall for the Republican lies in the last election, or that the Republicans were not more successful in suppressing the vote. Of course, that suppression was successful in 2014. Through the American system of gerrymandering (changing Congressional districts so one party will dominate), the Republicans still control the purse strings, and will see to it that the wealthy will continue to get a free ride, while they continue to blame the 47% for all the problems that face the nation. I am not a vociferous flag waving patriot, but frankly it makes me grateful every day to be a Canadian, because this is a country that has a heart and refuses to let ideology interfere with basic human rights so the poor can be portrayed as villains while the rich are given a free pass.

SUBMITTING TO THE AUTHORITY OF THE 1%

The American media, Democrats, Republicans and the Obama White House have nothing but words of disdain for what is going on in Syria. Secretary of State, Hillary Clinton, and President Barrack Obama are virulent in their condemnation of the brutal suppression going on there and in any other country where the authorities are suppressing mass demonstrations of people demanding freedom, unless, of course, it is a country like Saudi Arabia that is in the pockets of American oil conglomerates.

MUSINGS FROM THE EDGE: A COMPENDIUM OF THAT WHICH AFFLICTS THE HUMAN SPIRIT

Meanwhile, the absolute silence from the White House regarding the growing repression against peaceful demonstrators in the USA demanding economic justice receive not even the slightest mention from these so-called defenders of the common-man. This is typical for a country that is now named by the world's citizens as the greatest threat to peace.

The greatest economic turmoil since the Great Depression aroused those who see that there is no future for 99% of the people, as long as the 1% continues to write checks to politicians to purchase the government they want. Ironically, these protests in large cities are being suppressed primarily by Democratic mayors who are supposed to represent the common man.

Every government wants to maintain the façade of respect for the rights of its citizens. The security forces in Syria assert that they are only squaring off against foreign-backed militants attempting to utilize the demonstrations for nefarious purposes. In the U.S., the preferred bogeymen are unruly and ultra-radical elements whose only desire is to create chaos. Fox News commentators even go so far as to have the audacity to ask how all these people can afford to take time off work, when they should be asking why these people don't have jobs to go to in an economy that operates for the benefit of the few at the expense of the many. Multi-million dollars salaries for quasi-journalists makes them certified members of the 1%.

Any movement that tries to effectuate positive change for the average person will consistently be met by hostility, because the power structure dealing with the demonstrators and the corporate media that reports on it have a vested interest in maintaining the status-quo. Police will always say that they were provoked by the demonstrators. As you watch the campus cop at the University of California at Davis walk down the line pepper spraying sitting demonstrators who meekly submit to the act of a brutality by the jack-booted representative of the entitled class, it is obvious that the power structure will absolutely allow no dissent against the rule of the 1%.

The reality is that any effective movement designed to create social change will be met with hostility by those sworn to serve and protect the establishment. The police may try to justify their aggression as a response to provocation, but it is plain to see who actually comes to a protest to stir up trouble. They come in blue uniforms, bullet proof vests, helmeted visors down, guns cocked, with big sticks ready to bash in the heads of those who dare defy authority. Yet, they call the demonstrators provocateurs. Meanwhile, on the nightly news, you see footage of America's leaders decrying the brutal suppression of demonstrators in Egypt, Libya, Syria and other nations that they consider non-democratic as these hypocritical, arrogant buffoons degrade these nations while proclaiming every government should respect the rights of its citizens. This is the height of hypocrisy.

The actions of the police to suppress freedom of speech and assembly are not unique to despots in faraway places. This is embarrassing for the U.S. president, not only because his rhetoric about the right to protest is obviously empty, but also because of how close he is politically to the despots in the very countries he condemns for squelching free speech.

MUSINGS FROM THE EDGE: A COMPENDIUM
OF THAT WHICH AFFLICTS THE HUMAN SPIRIT

Mao once said that power comes from the barrel of a gun. The USA proves that every day all over the world with its corporate military machine. Unfortunately, they also prove it at home by dispatching police to brutalize their own citizens who are expected to submit to the will of the 1%. If power does indeed come from the barrel of a gun, maybe it is time for the demonstrators to realize that non-violence has never achieved any positive results for the masses. Those who think Martin Luther King changed things with his non-violence are living in a dream world. It was not non-violence that achieved civil rights for blacks in America. It was not until the cities of America went up in flames that the power structure finally decided that they had better make changes before the demonstrators wound up burning the suburbs.

It wasn't King who won the day, but Black Panthers toting AK 47's. Until the 99% start burning down Wall Street, corporate offices and the gated estates of the 1%, there will never be any appreciable change. It is time the 99% realized that change can only come through the complete overthrow of a system based on greed. Until the last privileged leech has surrendered to the authority of the masses, there will never be any economic equality. All power comes from the barrel of a gun, not from meekly submitting to the authority of the 1%. Revolution is not anarchy. It is an assertion of the right to life, liberty and the pursuit of happiness.

SUPPORTING THE PEOPLE
WHO ENSLAVE THEM

OK, here I go. It is once again time to explore the insanity of those south of us. I get e-mails from a variety of people in the United States of America, and many of them are anti-Obama, anti-government, anti-welfare tirades from those who think that government should not be there to protect the vulnerable in society. As typical of Americans, it is every man for himself. Do not offer a hand-up to those who suffer the misfortunes promulgated by a nation dedicated to the service of those at the top of the economic ladder.

What is even more frightening is that often these tirades are manifested by people who are teens or in their early 20's. It is apparent that the brainwashing of Americans to patriotic servitude and the worship of capitalistic greed applies to the younger generation as well as those older Americans.

For example, I received an e-mail that quoted a 21 year old female who is worried about social welfare and big government. She thinks if she is put in charge, she can take care of the problems, just like the other Republicans, by off-loading all the blame on those at the bottom of the economic ladder who are sponging off the hard-working Americans. My guess is that she is from an affluent family and would not know hard work if it bit her on the backside.

She would get rid of food stamps. Great idea. Why poor children should be allowed to eat. I suppose she is probably a Christian, too. Why? Because they are the people who rant and rave against abortion and free health care, but refuse to do anything for the children once they are forced into a world that will devour them as unworthy leeches. This is the kind of hypocrisy that abounds in America.

MUSINGS FROM THE EDGE: A COMPENDIUM
OF THAT WHICH AFFLICTS THE HUMAN SPIRIT

Furthermore, she would make those who do get welfare eat only rice and beans, rather than frozen pizza and steak. Frozen pizza is actually cheaper to feed a poor family than rice and beans. The reason there is so much obesity among the poor is because they cannot afford a healthy diet. Go into a grocery store sometime and look at the prices of fruits and vegetables. The poor cannot afford to eat healthy.

I do give her credit for one thing. She suggested Norplant Birth Control implants. Actually that is a good idea for the rich and the poor, but with Republicans in control of most state legislatures, good luck getting birth control and abortions on-demand as they must cater to their religious base. According to her, if you reproduce, you need to get a job. OK, I can go along with that, but if the poor don't reproduce where will the 1% get their slave labourers for their businesses, gardeners, maids, chauffeurs and nannies?

Then she suggested that all welfare recipients be tested for rugs, alcohol and nicotine. I can even agree with that, as long as the CEO's and bank presidents are included. Also, how about testing the affluent for their prescription drug habits?

Next, she decided that putting the poor in a military barracks, rather than government housing, would make them straighten up and act "white." This is a person who hates government interference in people's lives, but still comes out in favour of the government sticking its nose into what you do in your home. If you want an Xbox 360 or a plasma TV, she suggests you get a job. Yeah, try buying those items on a Wal-Mart slave wage.

MUSINGS FROM THE EDGE: A COMPENDIUM
OF THAT WHICH AFFLICTS THE HUMAN SPIRIT

Remember, this is a person who wants the government out of people's lives. Then she comes up with the idea that an individual must have a weekly pay-check or report for a "government" job. This is the kind of convoluted thinking that has those against Obamacare saying they don't want a government bureaucrat between them and their doctor, but it is alright to have a corporate CEO between you and your doctor. And this person thinks she can run things better?

She even goes further to say these people would be out on the roadways picking up trash, painting and repairing public housing. Once again, her solution involves the government she wants out of people's lives. Then she allows her abject racism to rear its ugly head by demeaning people with 22 inch tire rims (obviously Mexicans) and blasting stereo speakers (obviously African-Americans).

In a nation know for racism, maybe this should not be surprising at all. She justifies this immensely coercive cornucopia of fascism by stating that all this is completely voluntary. Yeah, like hating the Jews in World War II Germany was voluntary. You didn't have to hate them, but if you were seen aiding them you suffered the same fate as they did.

Then, she really goes over the top by saying " before you say that this would be demeaning and ruin their self esteem, consider that it wasn't that long ago that taking someone else's money for doing absolutely nothing was demeaning and lowered self-esteem. I wonder if George Bush doing nothing for eight years lowered his self-esteem? The rich and powerful seem to never have a

J. Wayne Frye

problem with self-esteem in America, because by virtue of birth they think of themselves as the "entitled class."

She even goes so far as to say the current system rewards those on welfare for bad choices. Yeah, like the bankers and Wall-Street barons I suppose. They were all rewarded for their bad choices, and this young lady has no problem with them stealing billions from the American public, nearly bankrupting the nation and destroying the retirement nest eggs of millions of old people.

Finally, she acts like a Republican governor instituting voter ID laws to lower the democratic voter turnout. She insists that she would not allow anyone on government subsistence to vote. Boy, she would have been right at home with the framers of the U.S. Constitution who denied women and slaves the right to vote. Then they went even further and stated that only land-owners had the right to vote – thus doing exactly what she wants – denying the right of the poor to take part in elections.

People like this heartless, uncaring young lady are why the USA is the laughing stock of the world as a nation of hypocritical, finger-pointing, brainwashed people who line up to be made slaves by their corporate masters. So once again, I say to my Canadian readers – be very leery of falling for any propaganda from America where the 1% continue to solidify their rule, supported by the very people they enslave.

THE CAPITALIST WILL SELL US THE ROPE WITH WHICH WE WILL HANG HIM

.

I have not owned a television for some time now. Yet,

without paying a cable company or a satellite provider, I see anything I want to watch commercial-free. I do not have to subject myself to the banal machinations of Madison Avenue always trying to brainwash me into buying products I do not need and cannot afford. The sense of freedom I feel is comparable to the feeling I got when I immigrated to Canada from the United States of America. Eight years ago I removed the shackles of an increasingly uncaring, religious, fascist, corporate theocracy and crossed the border into Canada, never looking back. A mere seven months ago, thanks to modern technology, I decided it was time for another declaration of freedom. So, I informed my satellite provider that I no longer needed their 450 channels of junk for which I was paying $82.50 per month. The freedom I feel is almost euphoric.

I now have over 20,000 channels I receive for free through the internet. Granted, I am paying $20.50 per month for internet service. (Yes, that is the cheapest in Canada and it is municipally owned, so there are no stockholders or high-paid executives to pay.) The service is comparable to any I have used since being here. Also, I would have internet anyway, so the cost is negligible.

I watch recent films within a few days after their release. What is more important, I am not relegated to watching the mindless pabulum put out by the corporate Hollywood junk purveyors who are more interested in box office revenue than providing quality entertainment. I see sub-titled French, German, Swedish and even Afghani films that do more than simply show car chases, gratuitous sex and gross humour. They actually have a message to convey. And thank goodness for the Indian movies. Bollywood (Mumbai, India) makes great movies the artistic way Hollywood did in the 1930's and 1940's, so I have no problem watching them with my grandchildren, as we can all comfortably watch films with some artistic merit that avoid profanity and simulated sex which seem an integral part of most Hollywood fare.

However, I am fearful, as the forces of evil are lurking about trying to control one of the last bastions of freedom left for humanity – the internet. The corporate barons of greed in the USA are already putting pressure on governments all over the world to cease the abomination of file sharing and video streaming that is cutting into the corporate bottom line. Just as the USA did with the copyright laws, arm-twisting every country to tie up copyrights almost in perpetuity for corporations, there is now a concerted effort by this nation that is a monument to greed to take away the freedom offered us peons by the internet. They want to make it possible for corporations to control what we are entitled to see. Freedom is always qualified by what is best for corporate interests and the people's rights be damned.

I am thankful I am an older person, because I will be one of the last human beings who remembers the freedom enjoyed by so many before the corporations, led by the USA, hijacked governments all across the globe and set out to enslave all of humanity to their insidious evil. So, while you can, free yourself from your cable or satellite provider and tune to some great old TV shows and movies at *Veetle* – my favourite site that fights the corporate media dominance. The internet may be corporate controlled, but remember what Lenin said, "the capitalist will sell us the rope with which we will hang him."

MUSINGS FROM THE EDGE: A COMPENDIUM
OF THAT WHICH AFFLICTS THE HUMAN SPIRIT

RISING UP IN ANARCHY

Remember that old Hank Williams'
tune about men with a broken heart?
About how people in pain had their souls
pierced with a melancholy dart.
I recall, as a youth, hearing it played incessantly
on an old Asheboro, North Carolina juke box,
Not realizing then, it was about a dream
crushed by a mountain of falling rocks.
Each day the world grows wearier
on each and every street,
As people wonder aimlessly about,
looks on their faces that portray defeat.
They are poor souls destroyed by a system
of servitude called capitalism,
Reflecting defeat like the rain clouds
peering through a prism.

These people have nothing left but a living death
that sears broken hearts
and captures their souls in servitude.
Caught in capitalistic hell,
all their possessions now in shopping carts.
How easy it is to rant, rave, ridicule and condemn.
Are we too stupid to realize that we could be them?

They put all their hope in a cruel system
that made their misery start,
Leaving them helpless in a system
that only knows how to break a heart.
Remember what Hank said about
humbling yourself when they pass by,
For it is written that the greatest men

J. Wayne Frye

MUSINGS FROM THE EDGE: A COMPENDIUM OF THAT WHICH AFFLICTS THE HUMAN SPIRIT

are never too big to cry.

Yet, the great in the land of broken dreams
have no compassion for those left behind.
The people at the top live in such excess
they no longer know what it means to be kind.
All hope has been dashed by
Ronald Reagan's culture of greed.
The legion of the defeated
no longer even have a dream.
The capitalist uses a sour dream
to manipulate and control.
In the end, all are discarded by their masters
into an insidious black hole.
All wealth flows to those at the top
with institutionalized impunity,
Because at the bottom there is no unity.
I am old and weary, no longer able
to see any hope to end the slavery
In a system that is manipulated and controlled
by an hierarchy of the unsavoury.
Will not the people finally end it all
by standing up to the economic oligarchy,
and demanding justice as they
rise up in unison causing
anarchy, anarchy, anarchy, anarchy, anarchy.

CHRISTMAS: SHAKE YOUR HEAD AND BAWL

Tis the night before Christmas
and all through the towns,

those with plenty shout with joy,
as only materialism abounds.
Yet, vast numbers are living

MUSINGS FROM THE EDGE: A COMPENDIUM
OF THAT WHICH AFFLICTS THE HUMAN SPIRIT

with their cupboards bare,
living in an economic system
based on greed that does not care.
There are children who
are begging for a call
of compassion from a society
that worships at the mall.

Then there are the older citizens
who beg on the streets,
wondering why the system
ignores them and yet achieves great feats.
Capitalism throws people out the back door
as if they were trash.
Those who are exalted are the ones
with great amounts of cash.
Now the discarded ones are lonely,
destitute and have no home.
The rich, with capitalistic disdain,
won't even throw them a bone.

Capitalist society blames the discarded
for their own plight.
They just wish there was some way
to keep poverty out of sight.
Still, the populace lines up
to give capitalism a cheer,
while ignoring the poor
like they are something to fear.
Most people lie down to sleep
and sweet dreams fill their heads.
Why shouldn't it be in a warm home
with queen sized cozy beds?
There is no thought for those

J. Wayne Frye

MUSINGS FROM THE EDGE: A COMPENDIUM OF THAT WHICH AFFLICTS THE HUMAN SPIRIT

on the outside looking in with tears
and longing for a hand of compassion
to quiet desperate fears
Like it was for Joseph and Mary,
there is no room in the capitalists' inn,
and no willingness to do that
which would fill the poors' bare food bin.
Jesus said to the rich,
"give all you have to the poor."
Ah, but the capitalists think
that Jesus was a bore.
Today, getting rich is preached
as a great and worthy trait.
Yet, there are a few of us
who won't swallow the bait.
Christmas is nothing more
than glorification of greed.
Ah, the capitalists have hijacked it
to plant their sinister seed.

Christmas is not a celebration
of the dear saviour's birth.
It is a time for the capitalists
to count money with great mirth.
Even non-believers have been
skilfully manipulated to spend,
Unable to fathom how capitalism
leads to a downward trend.

Christmas is joyous for the capitalists
who have hijacked the day,
because it is to the great God
of money they really pray.
For those who hope for a better day

when the table of plenty is set for all,
Christmas is nothing more than a reason
to shake your head and bawl.

My exposure to Top Secret information at the seat of deceit in the Pentagon during the Vietnam War taught me that the USA was a nation that had no core. Inside, liberty was actually empty and no heart of hope was beating for those who lacked power, prestige and privilege. Liberty for Americans was all talk and no action, unless, of course, the action entailed using the poor who serve in the military as cannon fodder to protect corporations by despatching a heartless military juggernaut to maintain control.

Up to this point, I have offered reasons for the world being used as a modern day concentration camp for the poor, who are walled off in ghettos of despair where they are offered little hope in rising from the ashes of the lives of desperation that they live as they are marginalized by the culture of greed.

Ironically, the middle class in America has been propagandized into believing that they are footing the bill through taxes for the poor people to live off government largesse. They simply are too engrossed in who sits atop the latest NCAA football poll, who will win the next Idol competition or what the latest antics of the Kardashians are to realize that the wealthy and the corporations are the ones getting the real welfare. Rather than worrying about the poor who struggle to find a decent paying job in a nation that refuses to raise the minimum wage to a living wage, they should be worried about how the rich, like the Koch brothers and the Walton family, are funding organizations that buy politicians so they can continue to

J. Wayne Frye

ignore environmental laws and utilize their power to pay slave wages and avoid a system of fair taxation. The middle class is brainwashed into believing it is the poor who are getting a free ride on their hard work and taxes, when it is really the rich who are getting the free ride by avoiding taxes and any social responsibility. You don't get wealthy on your own. It happens because people work hard for you so that you can realize profits..

Still, the propagandized masses salute the flag and put their right hands over their hearts when the National Anthem is played without realizing the whole thing is a giant charade of manipulation.

My eyes were opened because of an illegitimate, unnecessary war. After a short time, I realized that I had more in common with the Vietnamese peasants who were fighting me than I did with the over paid generals who told me I was defending freedom. I long for the day when the poor the world over unite, walk into the corporate owned grocery stores and start removing the food they need from the shelves. Until the poor get off their knees, until middle class realizes that they are on their knees, too, the rich and privileged will continue to control our lives. The time honoured tradition when people are oppressed is to rebel and I hope the day of rebellion is close at hand when the people united will stand against a system based on greed.

CHAPTER 4

LUNATICS ARE RUNNING THE ASYLUM

In the movie *Stonehearst Asylum*, the inmates take over the asylum and wind up doing a better job of running it than the professionals. I remember my grandfather once telling me that all the sane people were locked up and the really crazy people were running the government. He even went further by saying that prisons were full of people who refused to follow the rules and committed petty crimes like stealing to survive and that the real criminals were sitting in the banks and the board rooms stealing millions without paying for their crimes. Although he only had a 3rd grade education, he was an astute observer of how capitalism was used to keep people in bondage. He survived the Great Depression, which gave him a distinct insight on the depth of evil in a system that is based on greed. He was an entrepreneur who figured out how to survive, but he always had a soft spot for those who had to struggle to keep their heads above water. He was not rich in money, but when he died the funeral had the largest attendance in North Carolina history, because he touched people's lives with his kindness. He had no use for religion, as he said it was just a way to keep the poor in line by promising them a reward after death while the rich got their reward on earth, but ministers lined up to file past his casket, because they saw in him as a man who embodied the compassion that Christians are supposed to show. I was only 12 years old when he died, but I fondly remember a minister putting his arm around me and saying, "Your grandfather had no religion, but he put Christians to shame with his compassion."

That day is indelibly burned into my mind, because I actually never realized how respected and admired this simple man was. What greater epitaph can any of us have than "This was a compassionate person in a nation where everyone is taught to get what you can for yourself at all costs?"

My own father once told me, "Wayne, you'll never amount to anything in life, because you are too kind. Only the ruthless get to the top." I disagreed with my father many times, but I must admit that in a system based on greed, being ruthless does pave the road to success. However, if that is what it takes to be successful, I had rather be a failure. So, I now offer some prose that will hopefully tug at your heart and make you open up your arms and embrace economic justice.

SONG OF THE DESK/SONG OF THE FIELDS

Those who sit in their air-conditioned offices
at computer terminals, live in towers of denial.
They get off work, take the elevator
down to the parking garage,

MUSINGS FROM THE EDGE: A COMPENDIUM
OF THAT WHICH AFFLICTS THE HUMAN SPIRIT

get in their climate controlled Lexus automobiles
and drive past row after row of dilapidated homes
on their way out of the jungles of concrete and steel.

From behind their blackened privacy glass,
they look in disdain at people
in ragged clothes among piles of rubbish.
They zip past burned-out buildings,
and cruise up the on ramp,
leaving behind the megalopolis of despair.

They meander along the freeway and exit
into their suburban enclave,
of gated, protected, lily-white communities,
never acknowledging those who toil in obscurity.
They curtly wave at their Hispanic gardeners,
who load worn-out trucks with the implements
used to manicure and refine their high-priced lawns.

They push the garage door opener
and pull into the garage
next to the newly purchased grey mini-van.
Greeted at the door by an immaculately dressed,
blond, blue-eyed, shapely trophy wife,
these pillars of the executive community
hug their polite, mannerly children
and head for the 72 inch giant wall television
as they they prepare to relax on
their high-dollar, vibrating recliner.

These people are living the good life,
because they know that their labour is appreciated
and truly valued by a society of haves and have-nots
The paycheque they receive every two weeks

J. Wayne Frye

MUSINGS FROM THE EDGE: A COMPENDIUM
OF THAT WHICH AFFLICTS THE HUMAN SPIRIT

from their benevolent employer validates their worth.
Their contributions to society are rewarded
with perks that institutionalize their superiority.

These men go with their wives into
the well-stocked neighbourhood grocery
perfectly willing to pay the corporation
that owns the immaculately maintained store.
They readily accept having to pay the corporations
that package, market and distribute the vegetables and
fruits in their plastic grocery cart
They pay the charges to a part-time,
brown-skinned, minimum wage employee
who toils in a place she cannot afford to shop.

These people never give a thought
to those who work for meagre wages,
toiling in the dusty fields to pick
those vegetables and fruits.
They do not value their labour,
because it is not done in an air-conditioned office
by a man in a tie and pin-stripped suit.
Yet, it is these toilers of the soil
who are the real workers in America.
It is they who make good lives possible.
In a nation with a cornucopia of wealth,
should not these people get a slice of the pie?

ORWELLIAN TRUTH

Orwellian thought says:
Who controls the past, controls the future.
Who controls the present, controls the past.

MUSINGS FROM THE EDGE: A COMPENDIUM
OF THAT WHICH AFFLICTS THE HUMAN SPIRIT

So, in America, history is a lie.
The country was not founded for equality.
It was founded by rich farmers
Who wanted to be free of paying the English taxes.
That is why these slaveholding hypocrites said:
All men are created equal,
When what they meant was
That the wealthy should get
Free ride and avoid taxation.

Oh holy lie you shall not stand forever,
As the masses will one day walk inside lady liberty
And find she has no heart and is corrupted to the core.
The truth shall abound across a land that will see
The oppressed rise from their knees
And put their oppressors on theirs!

J. Wayne Frye

CHAPTER 5

LAND OF BROKEN PROMISES

The following speech was delivered in Los Angeles many times to young minority students who I always saw as the true element for change in a society that refuses to reach out to the less fortunate and offer real equal opportunity.

SEEK THE TRUTH

It is a privilege to be able to speak to you today on this special occasion. Your administrators have asked that I keep my remarks short in order to quickly facilitate the rapid conclusion of this gathering. However, I think the real reason may be that they are fearful of the things I might say. This is not an indictment of them as individuals, because they are a dedicated group of people whom I feel genuinely care about you and your education. We live in a society that is very tradition bound. Change is a word that causes great consternation to individuals in positions of power, and there are those in positions of authority who want to continue to keep you mired in the ghetto without hope for any thing other than a minimum wage or slightly higher job that will enslave all of you to serve at the lower rung of corporate America.

I once had a person tell me that the truth will set me free. Today, I am going to tell you the truth. You may not like what you hear, but I want all of you to be free, and if you are to be free, it is important that you know the truth. The truth has been hidden for too long from the average American. The privileged are fearful that if individuals like you ever know the truth, their positions of authority and privilege will come tumbling down like a house of cards.

The truth is simply that America never has been, and never will be the greatest nation on earth until it deals with the lack of social justice that is apparent every day in a society that allows some people in the wealthiest nation on earth to go to bed hungry at night. You live in a community filled with poverty and crime, not because you are bad, but because you are not deemed worthy to share in the promise that America has made for two-hundred years but never fulfilled. You are not created equal to the child in Beverly Hills, no matter what you are told. Furthermore, you can grow up to be President if you were born in this country, but how many of you really think that you have an equal chance of being President to the youth who lives in Beverly Hills?

How did I arrive at the conclusion that the United States is a country that is floundering in mediocrity while the rest of the industrialized world moves forward in bringing its citizens the social justice we all deserve? The answer can be found in books, newspapers, magazines and statistics available to all of you willing to make the effort to find the truth about a country that keeps its citizens fooled by manipulation and a steady diet of lies from its politicians and rich tax dodgers.

I am going to compare America to other countries, so that you can see for yourselves why we have nothing to be proud of in a country that has the largest percentage of its population living in poverty in the whole industrialized world. We are the only industrialized nation besides South Africa that does not provide its citizens with universal free health care. We spend more money on the military as a percentage of gross national product than any other country in the world. In fact, we spend three times as much as the next closest country. We have a stockpile of weapons of mass destruction that makes us potentially the greatest threat to world peace on this planet, but we think other nations should not have the right to stockpile these weapons to defend themselves from our insidious desire to gobble up the whole world in the name of corporate America. We are the only industrialized country that allows it citizens to own handguns with almost no controls whatsoever. We have the highest murder rate in the entire world, because we think guns are for protection rather than for killing. We have more people in prison than any other country in the world. We are the only industrialized country that still insists on having the death penalty, even though we have obviously executed innocent people. Finally, we are the only industrialized country in the world that allows religion to play an integral part in the way we conduct the affairs of government. This means very simply that we must bend public policy to the will of a pack of judgmental hypocrites who want to tell us all how to think and how to act. Is this the kind of country you want your children to inherit?

Let's take a brief look at another country that offers an excellent example of how social justice can be achieved even within the confines of a capitalistic system that very obviously leads to a class structure, but a class structure that is much less pronounced than it is in this country, where the gap between the haves and have-nots continues to widen.

The United States is proclaimed the greatest country in the world by Americans and immigrants from third world countries who do not understand that there are other countries in the world that far exceed the United States in offering its citizens the full fruits of a truly democratic society and the comfort of a country that is more economically just.

The United Nations issues rankings of countries every year based on quality of life and America continues to fall each year. It is now number fourteen in the quality of life ratings and continues to fall as it allows its citizens to go without quality, universal health care; decent access to education for all its citizens and uses an outmoded system of electing its leader that does not always allow the person with the most votes to win an election. For example President Bush who was appointed rather than elected, was a man who lost the election by over 500,000 votes, but still sat in the seat of power to protect the moneyed interests of those who made sure he was elected to provide the protection they needed in order to maintain their position of privilege. Canada, Norway, Finland, Sweden, Demark, France, Switzerland, Belgium,

J. Wayne Frye

Germany and the Netherlands came ahead, in that order, of the United States.

Since I am moving to Canada which ranked number one, I will not talk to you about that country today. Rather we will compare, very briefly, the number two country, Norway, with the United States. I am very familiar with Norway, because I spent four weeks there every January for three straight years as a professor and hockey coach. It is a country virtually devoid of poverty and violent crime is almost nonexistent. Unlike America, their citizens are basically guaranteed a minimum income to make sure that no one goes without the basic necessities of life. Consequently, there is no reason to commit crimes in order to make sure you have the things one needs to survive.

Education for Norwegians is guaranteed through college. Basic schooling is thirteen years, then the government will pay up to a certain amount based on your ability to pay for attendance at the college of your choice anywhere in the world.

The gap between the rich and poor in Norway is not as pronounced as it is in the United States, because they have system of taxation that makes the rich pay a fair share in taxes. In fact, once your income gets to a certain level the tax rate is seventy-two percent as those with more are expected to pay a fair share, rather than like America, where the rich top out at only thirty-four percent. This allows Norway to provide its citizens with a much more abundant life and makes for a predominantly middle class society as opposed to America where you have such a huge gap between those at the top and middle and an even more pronounced disparity between the rich and poor.

The control of citizen access to guns makes Norway one of the safest places in the world. In Norway, the King and Prime Minister do not even require bodyguards. In fact, the Prime Minister lives in an apartment rather than a huge taxpayer supported house like our President. There were only six murders in the country last year. The United States had nearly fifty thousand murders. What is it that makes America such a violent society when compared to other countries? Could it be our complete lack of respect for one another due to an intense emphasis in the pursuit of material possessions as the only route to happiness?

The final difference I want to cover today is health care. In America, the wealthy get the best care money can buy. Those of us who are less fortunate are relegated to the marginal hospitals. Some hospitals have even been known to let the uninsured die on the hospital steps waiting to be transported to a county hospital where they can get substandard treatment from less qualified doctors. In Norway, all citizens are guaranteed quality health care regardless of their income. Unlike America, where our public officials move to the head of the line and get the best health care in the world for free at the Walter Reed Army Hospital, in Norway, no one gets special treatment. Even the King and Prime Minister must go to public hospitals and they have to wait in line like everyone else. They have a much more equalitarian society than America.

This is only a brief exploration of the shortcomings of a society that has very little social justice, and will continue to keep you in bondage to the rich unless you stop falling for the propaganda they spout out to out to you as the truth. Stop being fooled by outright lies and half-truths. There are many countries in the world that offer a much more shining example of democracy and equality of opportunity than America. Do not fall victim to the manipulative flag-wavers who use patriotism as a cover to keep Americans enslaved to the privileged class. You can change the future, because you are the future. Seek the truth.

As a guest on a radio program to discuss the state of America's schools, Wayne delivered the following rebuttal to an individual who felt that poor people were getting what they deserved, because they tagged their schools with graffiti and were too unruly and undisciplined to get a decent education.

STORIES OF THE PAIN SUFFERED
BY THE UNEQUAL:

The following short stories represent the agony endured by those who must live in ghettos of despair, because they are not deemed worthy of the good life. This is my way of showing the personal cost of the inequality that an economic system based on greed causes. It shows the personal cost paid by those who are always on the outside looking in.

A society that ignores the plight of the most vulnerable while catering to the needs of the exalted will eventually fall under the weight of its own heartlessness. No other country is as heartless as the United States when it comes to the treatment of the poor.

MUSINGS FROM THE EDGE: A COMPENDIUM
OF THAT WHICH AFFLICTS THE HUMAN SPIRIT

SIRENS IN THE SLUMS OF DESPAIR

A siren wails in the distance as another testament to a youth who has fallen victim to the violence of poverty and disenchantment in a neighbourhood of despair surrounded by a city of affluence. The sound eerily penetrates the darkness, as I realize it is the sound of death. It vibrates in my ears seeming to say, "Death, death, death." I put my hands over my ears trying to blot out the horrors of it all, trying to muffle the sound that is so much a part of my life here. How do I blot out the noise of death?

THE SOUNDS OF PAIN
IN A HOME OF DARKNESS

Looking at my brother's room, it is hard to realize that I will never see him again. The baseball reminds me of his joy in doing something he loved. The computer reminds me of how devoted he was to learning so that he could escape this community of sorrow. The picture of him smiling with glee reminds me that he found joy while battling the demons of the streets that tried to suck the young life out of him and trap him in the darkness of despair. Finally, a stray bullet felled his hope along with his mother's. That is the pain of those who suffer the ills of a society based on greed.

The room is filled with reminders of a life that had promise, if only he could have survived the darkness that engulfs all who are isolated in the tyranny of poverty that abounds in the midst of plenty. It is so empty. It is empty of his smile, his laughter, the sound of a tennis ball bouncing against the wall and that clattering of computer keys as he typed his homework. The emptiness is

J. Wayne Frye

overwhelming. There is a void in the room that matches the void in my heart.

INJECTIONS OF PAIN

Looking down at the syringe lying in the alley, I wondered how John had gotten to the point that he let his addiction destroy him. He said it was the only way he could escape the pain of living a life of hopelessness while watching others live the good life almost in his midst.

The horror of it penetrates to the very depths of my soul as I look at that horrible needle that sucked the life, not only out of him, but out of those who loved him so dearly. Didn't he realize that every time he injected himself with that instant, liquid euphoria that he was only temporarily escaping from the realities of the dark existence foisted on him by a society in denial. Now, all of us who loved him are injected with the pain of carrying on without him.

THE DEAFENING SOUND OF SILENCE

As the policeman gingerly walked away, gliding slowly down the steps to avoid the trash thrown there by the junkies who milled about each day; I realized that there was not a sound to be heard. Silence abounded all around in a vacuum of misery. Even the gentle breeze that usually blew through the windows covered with sheets was strangely silent today. I looked out through the broken glass and saw no children playing in the streets. No doubt they had scurried inside yesterday when the bullets were whizzing all about, and their mothers would not let them back out today. This is life in an American ghetto which is nothing more than a modern day concentration camp for the poor in a nation that has no heart and no soul.

The silence was almost deafening. How can silence be so loud? My ears were penetrated with the pounding drumbeat of misery. I could not hear my son's voice. I could not hear his footsteps as he came down the hall to my room. It was over. All that was left was silence, the silence of death and the silence of the cold, dark, dampness of the grave. Finally the sound of silk, oh, the sound of silk touching silk as the coffin lid closed. The silence was too loud, too loud.

LAND OF BROKEN PROMISES

Guadalupe stood stoically in the raging rain, looking forlornly at Hector's dilapidated school. He would not be coming out the graffiti laden door again. He would not be running down the trash laden street to fondly greet her with his bountiful smile and warm embrace. He would not be walking home with her past alley ways filled with derelicts living in card board boxes. She would no longer have to protect him from the drug dealers who stood on street corners of despair selling escapism for the poor and hopeless. She would no longer have to fall over his body to shield him from the bullets that whizzed through the house on particularly violent Saturday nights. She would no longer have to explain to him why they could not afford a car. She would no longer justify being away from him to work two minimum wage jobs to pay-off the attorney who defended his dad on the robbery charge that sent him to jail for steeling groceries when they all lost their jobs. She would not have to tell him that his dad would be in jail for life since he had two prior convictions.

Why? Why was her son gone? Why had the dark, grim reaper come calling for a ten year old boy? Why did the bullet find him rather than the other children standing in front of the school? Why did this tall, grey, battered and dilapidated school building suddenly look like a tombstone, a grave marker for her little son who was silenced forever?

Looking at the building filled her heart with unbearable agony. It overwhelmed her until she dropped to her knees, sobbing with the pain inflicted on another mother who had fallen victim to the indifference that permeates a land of broken promises.

CHAPTER 6

A FINAL PLEA FOR COMPASSION

I once sat with my writing hero, the great storyteller and creator of the Mike Hammer mysteries, Mickey Spillane, at his rather modest home at Murrells Inlet, South Carolina. As he sipped on a beer, while my daughter and son played on his pier, he said, "Wayne, you may never sell that many books. Few people are as lucky as I am, but if you can reach people through a good, well-written story, you might just touch their hearts and show them a better path."

My life has often been an arduous journey, but the past few years as I have been able to devote more time to writing and enjoyed a modicum of success, I think of him often and how, although diametrically opposed to me politically, he helped me learn to weave a point of view into what I write. Sometimes you can show the heartlessness of capitalism with a simple story. Therefore, I shall conclude with what I hope illustrates the true nature of a system where the strong (economically well-off) prey upon the poor.

MUSINGS FROM THE EDGE: A COMPENDIUM OF THAT WHICH AFFLICTS THE HUMAN SPIRIT

RETURN OF THE BEAST

The lion rues the jungle.
Man rules the city.
But which is truly the beast?

Dan Pierce and Peter Levin had been working for two years in East Africa with the Global Telephone Company, stringing lines across the continent from south to north. Now, at the end of 1951, they were nearly to the north connecting point as they set up camp in the area that ws called Tsavo, Kenya. In a few days, their job would be finished and they could turn their backs on the teeming jungles of snakes, lions, monkeys, swarming insects and unfriendly natives to head back to the jungles of concrete and steel in New York City and Philadelphia, their respective homes.

They had a work crew of about fifty natives to assist in the stringing of poles and lines through the harsh Tsavo area. Dan knew that Tsavo meant "a place of slaughter" in the Swahili language. It had certainly lived up to that name in 1898, when two man-eating lions killed 140 railway workers in a barbaric rampage that made locals still afraid of the area, because the lions' spirits were believed to still roam the jungle.

Actually, the last one-hundred kilometres had been rather easy. There were no longer any lions in this part of Kenya. After those two man-eaters were killed by the renowned Colonel John Patterson, slaughter of lions by locals and hunters from Europe and America, plus the erosion of the soil as a result of over grazing by the big white-owned cattle ranches had turned the area into a wasteland, unable to sustain almost any kind of wild-life or human.

So Dan and Peter went about their jobs in a care-free manner as they had finally arrived in an area where they did not have to be as vigilant in guarding against a sudden attack from beasts. Their cavalier attitude was short-lived.

That very night, a lion carried off one of the native workers who wandered into the brush behind the camp. Dan and Peter followed the sound of the screaming, but lost the man-eater in the darkness. The last sound they heard was a horrible gurgling out in the heavy brush, then silence, deathly silence.

They figured the lion had wandered up from the south, where lions were more numerous. It was probably getting old, and like so many of the old in the world, it could no longer run-down its natural prey. Other members of the den probably refused to share any kills, looking on him as no longer useful, something that needed to be discarded and forgotten. Like an old man, weathered and broken by years of labour, the lion was no longer able to compete with the younger, more vigorous hunters.

Both men knew that unless the lion was killed, the camp would be in constant danger. Finally, after three days of searching, they assumed the lion had moved on. Things in the camp returned to normal as everyone got back into their routines, and the work was progressing at a rapid pace.

As the two men relaxed in Dan's tent, they discussed how their battles in the jungles of Africa were easy compared to their battles in the city slums, where they were both brought up in an environment of drug dealers, pimps, homelessness, violence and crippling poverty. They had experienced the jungles of America which were just as dangerous as Kenya's jungles.

Pete left Dan's hut and headed for his own. Who knows what strange Gods rule the night, the night that for so many can be never-ending? Night sheltered the lurking creatures of dismay, torment and death. Night can engulf you in the embrace of evil.

Pete removed his clothes, leaned his rifle against a box close to the tent opening, turned off the lamp and crawled into bed. He lay under the mosquito net, listening to the eerie quiet. He heard the faint rustling sound of the brush that surrounded the camp blowing in the light breeze. Then he heard a monstrous roar in the distance, the kind of roar that reminded him of the slum where he spent his childhood nights, listening the distant sounds of screams from people who were victims of the predators that roamed the city. He dropped off to sleep.

It was some time after 2:00AM when he awakened, but he wished he had continued sleeping. With his wakening breath, he detected the odour of a lion. It was a sharp, penetrating smell that pierced through his nostrils and hit the pit of his stomach like a huge wave on some far and distant shore.

He almost screamed, but guided by the urge for self-preservation, he realized that his only hope lay in remaining silent and still. The least sound or movement could mean instant death.

MUSINGS FROM THE EDGE: A COMPENDIUM OF THAT WHICH AFFLICTS THE HUMAN SPIRIT

His eyes became blurred, and sweat trickled down from his forehead. The lion was sniffing its way along the bed, baffled and confused by the mosquito net. Pete blinked his eyes and focused on his gun. Maybe he should make a try for it. "No," he thought. It is too far away. The lion would be on him before he was out of bed.

Pete took a deep breath and prepared to die as a giant paw ripped open the mosquito netting. Before he could move, savage, fanged teeth sank deep into his shoulder, and he was dragged onto the tent floor.

Blood streamed from his mutilated shoulder and neck. Still, he did not make a sound. For some reason, his ability to scream was numbed by the terror unfolding in his tent.

The lion let out satisfied grunts as it lapped up the blood. Pete prayed for his consciousness to subside, so he could be spared the agony of watching himself be torn to shreds by this wicked beast of the night.

Death was crouched over him, and like so many people who face turmoil and pain, he was helpless. How could he overcome the situation in which he had been unwillingly thrust? Was there a way to battle out of this predicament like he had battled to escape the pangs of despair suffered by that little boy from the slums of New York? Was there to be no escape? Was this lion a god of the night, sent to destroy all those who dare enter his domain? Inside Pete a voice kept saying, "Make an effort, make an effort to save yourself." Yet, the despair of his situation was overwhelming him. He was almost paralyzed with fear.

J. Wayne Frye

MUSINGS FROM THE EDGE: A COMPENDIUM OF THAT WHICH AFFLICTS THE HUMAN SPIRIT

He tried to get up on one knee. The lion whipped out a paw and with lightning fury exposed the bone on Pete's upper left leg. A vein spurted blood as it dangled from his lower hip, and as if angered by the action, the lion let out a deafening, blood-curdling roar.

The camp exploded with screams and shouts. There was the bellowing noise of a human stampede as natives scrambled out of their huts into the trees in search of safety from the devil who had come calling in Tsavo, the place of slaughter.

Dan, with chaos surrounding him, snatched up his rifle and headed for Pete's tent. With no moon and no campfire lighting, Dan groped tediously through the darkness.

Pete's consciousness had narrowed to one terrifying reality, the horrible lapping sounds of the brute as he licked blood from the gapping wounds.

The frantic noises outside caused the lion to cease its feasting. Sinking its teeth deep into Pete's shattered left shoulder, the lion leaped out of the tent into the blackness of the night, half dragging; half carrying Pete's mangled body.

> The lion rules the jungle.
> Man rules the city.
> But which is truly the beast.

Dan stumbled into the hut and managed to light a lamp. The blood stained bed and the torn flesh scattered around the tent made him temporarily close his eyes. Realizing immediate action might save his friend; he called to the natives to make torches and follow him in pursuit of the menacing devil that had once again brought terror to Tsavo, but only two among the multitude were brave enough to follow him into the bush. The others scurried out of camp, heading back to their villages proclaiming that the devil was once again roaming the plains of Tsavo.

Indeed it did appear that the darkness of the former terror was again wrapping itself around this place. Was there no place safe from the beasts that prey on the weak and innocent? Or was this beast just a victim of circumstances forced to ravage the unsuspecting for survival?

As if Pete were weightless, the lion carried him through the increasingly dense dry foliage, without pausing in its blood banquet. When the flesh became dry in one place, he would drop Pete to the ground, bite savagely in a new location and start his ghoulish lapping again.

How Pete stayed conscious was a complete mystery to him, but he prayed for death to save him from the horrors of the night. This beast was another in the long line of beasts that he remembered from a childhood filled with beasts that preyed on him and his loved ones in another kind of jungle. He realized that his escape was only illusionary, for now he was back in the jungle, struggling to survive the brutality of another form of beast.

The lion paused in the clearing and released its savage hold. As Pete rolled to his right, his left arm brushed the lion's paw. Harassed by the movement, the lion sank its teeth into what was left of Pete's forearm and bit it off at the elbow. When reflex reaction caused Pete's left leg to jerk, savage claws slashed viciously at it until only bone was left below the knee.

Pete cried to himself, "Oh God, when will I be given the gift of death to free me from this demonic world that rages about me?"

The lion sunk its teeth back into a tattered shoulder, and continued on its journey. Reaching the base of a huge tree sprouting large dead braches that thrust into the sky , seeming to touch the stars, the lion somehow managed to pull Pete's body into the tree, finally settling in a large branch about twenty feet above the ground.

The lion once again resumed its carefully placed biting and lapping, preparing the kill for the final feast. The only problem was Pete had to endure it all, because death continued to be denied.

The long, rough tongue scraped up Pete's thighs and stomach. As the great head of the burly beast neared Pete's face, he vomited from the loathsome breath that reached him in sickening gusts. The lion continued to lick steadily, closer and closer to Pete's throat. Instinct caused Pete to raise his remaining arm to protect his face. With an angry grunt, the lion bit off three fingers. His hand was in the lion's mouth, but instead of biting it off, he was content to suck blood from the mutilated hand. The darkness seemed to be closing in now as Pete felt that death surely had to come soon. How much longer could he survive in the grip of this evil beast of prey?

The lion rules the jungle.

J. Wayne Frye   129

MUSINGS FROM THE EDGE: A COMPENDIUM
OF THAT WHICH AFFLICTS THE HUMAN SPIRIT

Man rules the city.
But which is truly the beast?

Unknown to Pete, Dan, helped by the two torch-bearers, was making a frantic effort to find him. The three men moved through the prickly foliage cautiously as they neared the tree which served as Pete's earthly hell. Then in the flickering torch-light, they saw the vague outline of the lion as it crouched over Pete.

The two natives put out their torches and Dan edged his way toward the tree. As he came closer, the lion stopped its feasting and lifted its gigantic head to let out a warning growl.

Dan continued to close the distance until there was only ten feet separating him from the beast. Dropping to one knee, he aimed and fired. The bullet buried itself into the heavy fur, but the killer was not to be denied. Seemingly unfazed by the bullet wound, the lion leaped from its perch, and Dan Pierce struggled beneath its weight while the two natives dropped their torches, sitting the brush on fire, and bounded into the night like a flock of geese scared by a gun shot.

Dan Pierce had absolutely no chance. The giant beast slashed a paw across the right side of his head with such force that the skull gave way and brains spilled onto the ground next to his right eye that had been ripped from its socket by the large molars the lion furiously dug into Dan's face.

His lust for blood satisfied, the lion bounded victoriously from its ravaged victim and raced up the side

J. Wayne Frye

of a nearby hill. Like a great God of the jungle, he raised his head to the heavens and let out a deafening roar.

Meanwhile, Pete Levin had managed to raise his torn and tattered body to a sitting position. As he gasp for breath, blood streamed like a raging river out of his torn and lacerated mouth. He waited, waited for the return of the beast that stalks us all.

THE END

9 781928 183051